PURITAN PAPERBACKS

Searching Our Hearts in Difficult Times

John Owen

1616–1683

John Owen was born in 1616 in Stadhampton, Oxford-
shire and died in Ealing, West London, in 1683. During
his sixty-seven years he lived out a life full of spiritual
experience, literary accomplishment, and national
influence so beyond most of his peers that he continues
to merit the accolade of 'the greatest British theologian
of all time.' Despite his other achievements, Owen is
best famed for his writings. They are characterized by
profundity, thoroughness and, consequently, authority. Although many of his works were called forth by
the particular needs of his own day, they all have a
uniform quality of timelessness.

John Owen

Searching Our Hearts
in Difficult Times

Abridged and Made Easy to Read

THE BANNER OF TRUTH TRUST

THE BANNER OF TRUTH TRUST

Head Office
3 Murrayfield Road
Edinburgh
EH12 6EL
UK

North America Office
PO Box 621
Carlisle
PA 17013
USA

banneroftruth.org

These discourses and sermons are taken from
John Owen, *Works*, Vol. 9, (London: Banner of Truth, 1965),
in which they bear the original titles:
1. Several Practical Cases of Conscience Resolved, delivered
in some short discourses at church meetings
2. A sermon on Perilous Times, 2 Tim. 3:1
3. Four sermons on The Use and Advantage of Faith:
(i) in a time of public calamity
(ii) under reproaches and persecutions
(iii) if popery should return upon us
(iv) in a time of general declension in religion, Hab. 2:4

The text has been modernized.

*

ISBN:
Print: 978 1 84871 881 4
Epub: 978 1 84871 882 1
Kindle: 978 1 84871 883 8

*

Typeset in 11/14 pt Adobe Garamond Pro
at The Banner of Truth Trust, Edinburgh

Printed in the USA by
Versa Press, Inc.,
East Peoria, IL

Contents

Part II:
Difficult and Dangerous Times

Part III:
Living by Faith in Difficult Times

The use and advantage of faith:

PREFACE

I N his sermon at the funeral of John Owen, David Clarkson said of him:

> It was his great design to promote holiness in the life and exercise of it among you. But it was his great complaint that its power declined among professors. It was his care and endeavour to prevent or cure spiritual decays in his own flock.

This book exhibits some of the means by which Owen sought to 'prevent or cure spiritual decays in his own flock'. It is a paraphrase and modernization, with a very few slight abridgments, of three items (taken from volume 9 of his *Works*), all of which were published posthumously.[1] Owen had gathered a congregation in London from about 1667 onwards to which he ministered until his death at the age of 67 in August 1683.

1. Searching our hearts

This was originally entitled *Several Practical Cases of Conscience Resolved*, and was published in 1721. Owen would occasionally hold church meetings for spiritual conference

[1] *Works*, Vol. 9 (London: Banner of Truth Trust, 1965), pp. 358-405; 320-34; 490-516.

and fellowship at which various topics were addressed. These fourteen discourses were given as concluding summaries at the close of such discussions, or as preparatory talks before periods of corporate prayer. The questions discussed span the period between January 1672 and February 1680.

2. Difficult and dangerous times

This item was originally a sermon entitled *Perilous Times*, preached in 1676 and published in 1721.

3. Living by faith in difficult times

Owen entitled this series of four sermons *The Use and Advantage of Faith*. The series was preached in 1680 and published in 1756.

It should be noted that all the discourses in this book were delivered during the eight-year period between 1672 and 1680 and that they are therefore the product of Owen's later years. The various items were not prepared by Owen for publication but were produced from notes taken by a member of his congregation.

* * *

The condition of the Christian church in Britain and in America in the period between the end of the Puritan movement and the awakening associated with the Methodist revival (that is, the period from about the 1670s to the 1750s) was similar in many ways to that condition which has prevailed in these two countries from at least the 1950s onwards. During both eras the spiritual life of the two nations declined (with respect to whatever criteria one might employ). There were fears then, as there are now, that true religion would die out altogether. The well-known comment of Bishop Butler in 1736 seems ever more appropriate for our own days (that is, as far as Western civilization is concerned):

> It has come to be taken for granted that Christianity is no longer a subject of inquiry; but that it is now at length discovered to be fictitious. And accordingly it is treated as if, in the present age, this were an agreed point among all persons of discernment, and nothing remained but to set it up as a principal subject for mirth and ridicule.[2]

What is evident on a first reading of these short chapters therefore is the relevance of Owen's words to believers at the beginning of the twenty-first century. Foreseeing the desperate days that were in store for the church, he addressed the issues that would soon exercise the members of his own church, but his pastoral comments are just as helpful to us over three hundred years later. He considers experiences which are crucial in the life of the individual believer in every age – sin, conversion, assurance, prayer, faith, etc, but then, increasingly, he concentrates on those that arise in the life of a church or a nation at specific periods of spiritual decay and unbelief: backsliding, God's warnings, days of judgment. He stresses in particular the need of the individual Christian to identify with his nation in grieving and repenting over its

---

[2] Preface to Joseph Butler, *The Analogy of Religion* (1736).

sin. In all these various areas of Christian experience, Owen's warnings and counsels are piercingly honest, discerning and timely, and full of practical advice.

THE PUBLISHERS
July 2019

PART I:
SEARCHING OUR HEARTS

1. Conviction of sin before conversion

Question: *To what extent should I be convicted of my sin and guilt before I may turn to Jesus Christ to find salvation?*

Answer: The question relates to the least degree of sincere conviction that we must experience before we feel we have a right to come to Christ. What has been said today by some is very true, but others of you may have been discouraged on hearing it because you do not feel that your conviction of sin has been so definite or so full. We know that conviction is absolutely necessary, and so some of you might be thinking, 'What has been discussed is so much above anything that I have felt.'

I would not wish to say anything that would discourage anybody, so let me explain what I judge to be the minimum requirement—what I consider to be absolutely necessary—before someone can come sincerely to Christ. I must be careful not to undermine the souls of any, nor, on the other hand, to be unfaithful to the truth of God.

Whatever Jesus Christ requires of us in order that we believe in him, that is what is absolutely necessary from us; and I can show what this is from two or three scriptures.

(i) 'I came not to call the righteous, but sinners to repentance' (Mark 2:17).

To call sinners to repentance is to call them to repentance by faith in Jesus. Paul says 'The saying is trustworthy and deserving of full acceptance, that Christ came into the world to save sinners' (1 Tim. 1:15). What kind of sinners does Christ call? Those whom he calls to repentance, he calls to faith; and those whom he calls to faith so that they might believe, these are described as sinners—they are the opposite of 'the righteous'. 'I came not to call the righteous, but sinners' (Luke 5:32). Who, then, are these righteous? The Scriptures tell us that there are two kinds of righteous people. The first are those who believe that they are righteous in themselves, and who look down on other men. Any man who trusts in himself that he is righteous will never be called by Christ to believe. So long as a man thinks that he is good enough of himself, that he has nothing to fear, that man has no right or warrant to believe. The second case is the man described in another context by Paul as one who is 'ignorant of the righteousness that comes from God and seeking to establish his own' (Rom. 10:3). He might acknowledge that he is not perfect but he looks to gain righteousness by performing the works of the law, i.e. he goes about establishing his own righteousness. Now, Jesus Christ does not call such people as these to believe either; these righteous people have no right to believe. Who then does he call? 'Lost sinners,' says Christ, 'you are those whom I call to faith.'

This, therefore, is what is absolutely necessary to come to Christ: to be quite convinced that you are a sinner as to your state and your behaviour; that you are not righteous in yourself, and have no hope of being righteous in yourself. If a man is not really convinced that he is not righteous, he is not under the call of Jesus Christ. But if someone does believe this, he is under a sovereign dispensation, and such a person should never despair.

(ii) 'Those who are well have no need of a physician, but those who are sick' (Matt. 9:12).

As I understand it, there are two things for which a sick person goes to a doctor. The first is that he is uneasy. A man who is sick might put up with the illness, yet his uneasiness will make him visit the doctor. And Christ said, 'I came for those people who cannot find any rest or ease in their present condition.' Perhaps they have often tried other remedies and have found that nothing helps—they are still sick; their conscience is pricking them, their heart is burdened, and they have to find relief or they will never be free. Then secondly, there is the fear that the illness might be fatal. This certainly sends a sick person to the doctor. When the soul is made uneasy in its state and condition and can find no rest or ease, it thinks, 'If I stay like this, I shall be lost forever.' This is the soul that Christ calls; this man will place himself in the doctor's care, whatever the cost.

(iii) 'Come to me, all who labour and are heavy laden, and I will give you rest' (Matt. 11:28).

3

Here is a soul experiencing a great need and labouring for something by which it may be accepted with God. Very often such a person will try to keep from sin, will strive to fulfil Christian duties and will have strong desires to be acceptable to God. And what will be the result of all these strivings and efforts? He will be labouring and weary; that is, everything will prove completely ineffective. He is not able to find rest and peace and acceptance with God.

And now comes the turning point: (iv) 'You were wearied with the length of your way, but you did not say, "It is hopeless"' (Isa. 57:10).

When a soul has been labouring for acceptance with God and has become completely weary then Christ says to it, 'Come to me.' 'No,' says the light of nature, 'come to me; trust in your own efforts.' One person might reply, 'I will continue to see what I can do; I will not say, "There is no hope."' But another one will answer, 'I will not respond in that way. In my own strength all is hopeless. I will go to Christ.' That second man is the man whom Christ calls.

Now these are the things that I consider indispensably necessary if a person is to believe. I hope they are to be found in all of us, here today. And if so, we do not need to keep asking whether we were sincere in coming to Christ. I would not dare to argue that anything more is needed. Many pretend to believe, but they have never been thoroughly convinced that they are not righteous: they were never sick; they never had fears that they might die. They are the opposite of the express rule given by Christ: 'I came not to call the righteous, but sinners.' Sinners!—not those who say, 'There is hope,' but rather, those who sigh, 'There is no hope.'

2. Assurance of salvation

Question: *The act of being united with Christ is secret and hidden, and the times and seasons of their conversion to God are unknown to most people. What, therefore, are the evidences and signs for us to be certain that we have gladly and sincerely received Christ and returned to God?*

Answer: This question covers a large area, and it would be difficult to answer fully because of everything that is involved. I shall therefore refer to just a few things that, to my mind, are evidences of a sincere coming to and receiving of Christ—things that I know have been of help to many.

(1) One good evidence is a steadfastness and perseverance in the choice we make of Jesus Christ, notwithstanding the opposition that we shall meet with for making that choice. I am not going to refer to the circumstances or the thoughts and experiences that led up to our trusting in him, but (to the poorest and weakest of the flock that may be worrying whether or not they have a true belief in Christ) I say that they may judge whether they have believed by the continuation and perseverance of their choice against all opposition.

There are two sorts of opposition that will try us out and shake us, as I have found (if I have any true experience of these things): (a) Opposition from attacks of the conscience and the law with respect to the guilt of our sin. (b) Opposition from temptations to sin.

(a) Even after truly believing and coming to Christ there will be many heavy attacks made against a soul by the law and by the guilt of sin felt by the conscience. In such circumstances the crucial question is, 'On what does the soul depend when attacked in this way?' If someone is depending only on a conviction of sin, only on the fears and resolutions brought about by a sense of guilt, they will be very ready to find relief from another direction. They may have started their voyage well; a storm arises; the ship will not carry them; they must change direction for another harbour. I have known this happen with some, and I have known for myself when troubled by such crosswinds in my own soul—when I have felt the weight of the accusations of guilt and sin—that the soul finds it very hard to keep its hold. It may resolve, 'I will trust to Christ,' yet it may begin again to depend on self. It may begin to waver: 'I must remedy this. I must work out for myself a relief from this. I cannot withstand this attack by living wholly upon Christ alone. Afterwards, when the storm is over, I will venture out to sea again.' Such behaviour is not a good sign. But when a soul under these attacks which sometimes arise will not move from its position: 'Here I will trust in Christ, let the worst come upon me,' this is a persevering in our choice of Jesus Christ. I hope you have experience of it.

(b) We must persevere in our choice of Christ against temptations to sin as well as against the accusations of conscience. Bearing the load of accusations is truly a daily work. On occasions it can prove the heaviest burden we bear and it is always present to some degree or other. But what about temptations to sin? These may be temptations to neglect a duty, or to compromise with some evil way (to which we are subject while in the body), or it may be a temptation to some great evil. In these cases an answer similar to Joseph's, and applied to Christ, is a great evidence of the sincerity of our choice of Christ: 'How can I do this great wickedness and sin against God?' (Gen. 39:9). When a soul can draw a powerful argument from being tempted, by saying: 'How then can I do this, and still hold on to Jesus Christ? I will not do this against him whom I have chosen,'—this is a good sign that our trust in Christ is sincere.

(2) Growing in love towards the person of Christ is a great evidence to me of a sincere faith in Christ. This is a subject of great blessing but I shall only hint at a few things. When a soul has received Christ it cannot but study Christ. It is not a great argument against the sincerity of a man's faith and grace if he spends more time considering the *offices* and *graces* of Christ and the *benefits* that we obtain from him, but it is an argument against his growth in grace. A thriving faith and an increase in grace will show themselves in an increasing consideration of the *person* of Christ. This involves the soul studying his person, the glory of God in him, his natures, the union of them in one person, his love, condescension and grace. It involves the heart being drawn out to love him and to cry, 'Indeed, I count everything as loss because of the surpassing worth of knowing Christ Jesus my Lord' (Phil. 3:8). 'What is your beloved more than another beloved?' 'My beloved is radiant and ruddy, distinguished

among ten thousand… he is altogether desirable' (Song of Sol. 5:16). To see an excellence and a desirableness in the person of Christ so as to grow in admiration and love of him is, for me, an evidence that, when all else fails, will greatly support the soul and persuade it that its choice is true.

Indeed, it is one of the most spiritual of evidences, because I very much doubt if an unregenerate man can love Christ for his own sake at all. It is a true sign of growth when our love to the person of Christ grows, when we meditate much upon it, and when we think much about it. I could show you where it is that the beauty of Christ's person may be found, but I do not have time to do it now.[1]

(3) Another evidence, I believe, of a soul having made a sincere choice of Christ is when it continues to approve, judge well of, and appreciate more and more every day, the glory, the excellence, the holiness and the grace of the way of salvation by Jesus Christ. And this approval of the way of salvation is not only because it is the only way that offers escape from an otherwise unavoidable damnation, but also because it is such an excellent way: pardoning sin freely by means of Christ's atonement and the imputation of his righteousness to us, and at the same time glorifying the righteousness, holiness and grace of God.

What a blind, wretched creature I was, says the soul, that I did not see the wonder of this way before! It is far better than the way of the law and the old covenant. I

---

[1] Those wishing to take up this offer will find a very full exposition in *Meditations and Discourses on the Glory of Christ* in Owen, *Works*, Vol. 1 (London: Banner of Truth Trust, 1965), pp. 273-415.

approve of it with all my heart. If there were any other possible ways presented before me, I would choose this way—going to God by Jesus Christ—as being the best way, the way that brings most glory to God, most satisfaction to the creature, and is most suited to the desires of my heart. I would have no other way. 'I am the way, the truth and the life,' says Christ (John 14:6), and this is what I will stay with, whatever happens to me. Though I should perish, I will stay with it, since God has shown to me that its glory, that of the salvation of sinners by Christ, is greater than any other glory, other than that of heaven. I see such a glory to God in it, such an exaltation of Christ, whom I love, such an honouring of the Holy Spirit, and such safety to my own soul, that I will stay with it.

An increase in our approbation of the way of salvation gives some assurance that we have made a true and sincere choice of Christ.

Allow me to add one other thing: (4) A delight in obedience to God by Christ in the ways that he has appointed for us, is a great evidence that we have chosen Christ, and he us. The true ways to worship God in his church and ordinances are those ways of worship that Christ has appointed. If these things are judged in the abstract, in and of themselves, we might be tempted to say of them, as was said of Christ, 'There is no beauty or glory in them that we should desire them' (Isa. 53:2). There is much more outward beauty and glory in other ways that Christ has not appointed. But if we love the ways that Christ has appointed purely because he has appointed them, then we choose them because we have chosen him to be our king. This is what gives them beauty and life. And if the ways of Christ's appointment begin to grow heavy and become a burden to us, if we are weary of them and would wish to have our necks free from under the yoke, then that is a sign that we are growing weary of him who is their author. This is a sure sign that we never made a true and right choice of him.

I might offer many other things as evidences of a sincere trust in Christ but these are some which have been of use to me, and I hope that they may be so to some of you.

3. The sins of our day and age

Question: *What part do we have in the sins of the day and age in which we live?*

Answer: All sins come under two headings—Unbelief, and Immorality

(1) *Unbelief.* This also may be reduced to two headings—atheism and false worship. This second heading contains, in particular, the contempt of all instituted worship and involves the many sins that arise from the breaking of the commandments of the first table of the law. However, presently, I shall speak only of the first heading.

It may be that no age can compare with ours for atheism, when we consider all the ways in which the atheism of man's heart manifests itself. The source of it is to be found only in the heart of man. 'The fool says in his heart, "There is no God"' (Psa. 14:1). The heart is the seat of atheism. Consider the ways in which it reveals itself:

(a) By horrid, cursed, blasphemous swearing—which is a contempt of the name of God. And when was it ever more prevalent in our nation than now?

(b) By the reproaching of the Holy Spirit of God. Perhaps this is the particular sin of the nation today, not known or heard of to such an extent in any other nation under the sun.

(c) By mocking all holy things: the Scriptures; everything that involves a reverence and a fear of God—so that a man who acknowledges that his actions are governed by the fear of God automatically receives the scorn of all around him.

(d) By the contempt of all God's providential warnings. No nation has ever received more warnings from God's providence, nor were these ever more despised than they are today.

These things, brothers, are not done in a corner; they are perpetrated in the face of the sun. The mist from them darkens the whole heavens and they increase more and more every day.

(2) *Immorality*. It would be an endless work to list all the sins that reign among us—cruelty, violence, uncleanness, sensuality, drunkenness—all raging and reigning to their utmost in the nation. I mention these things as matters that should be a grief to us before God, and should affect us whenever we think of them.

To this great predominance and prevalence of sin in the whole nation must be added an awful sense of *security*. The truth is that at one time the people of this land were awakened a little. When God's judgments were upon us—the plague, the fire, and, a year later, another warning[1]—there was a degree of quickening, like a man awaking from a dead sleep, lifting his head and rubbing his eyes for a few moments. But having observed something of the world now for about forty years, I can testify that I never saw our land in such a complacent security as it is at present. In former days there were continual warnings that God had a quarrel with the nation and those that feared God spoke to one another about it, and we saw and discovered that these warnings were not empty words. But now, today, there is just a general sense of security. Men complain of adversities, needs, poverty and so on, but as far as anything to do with God's involvement in the world is concerned, either my judgment deceives me or I never saw the land so complacent and at ease. And this indifference has affected us all, even the churches of God themselves.

These things are a matter of fact. The question is: Are we to be greatly concerned over these things or not? They are the sins of wicked men and of the persecutors of God's people. What have we to do with them?

The psalmist of old said that, his 'eyes shed streams of tears, because people do not keep your law' (Psa. 119:136). And you know that God has set a mark of approval, not on those who are free from the sins of the age, but on those who groan over the abominations that are in our midst (Ezra 9:4). It will not be sufficient for us merely to be free from such

[1] A reference perhaps to the riots that broke out in many parts of the country in 1667, provoked by unemployment and high taxation; or possibly to the Dutch navy raid that sailed up the Thames in June 1667 and humiliated the British navy by towing away *The Royal Charles*, the flagship of the fleet, and sailing her back to Holland.

sins unless we are found to be those who groan over them also. Brothers, our own hearts know that we are guilty in this matter and that we need to seek God's face today that he would give us a deeper sense of these things than we feel at present. The name of God is blasphemed; the Spirit of God reproached; a flood of iniquity spreads itself over the land, the land of our birth, the inheritance of Christ, over a nation professing the reformed religion. All these things are retrograde; everything is in declension. Indeed, brothers, if you will not acknowledge this, I will do so, before you all, and to my own shame, that I bear much guilt in this respect, and that I have not been so aware of the sins of the nation so as to mourn for them and be humbled over them as I should have been. And it would be good for you to search your own hearts and examine your own position, whether you have truly been affected by these things, or whether you have thought that everything is well merely because all is well with your own family and, perhaps, with our own church. The carelessness and lack of apprehension that is upon the nation is a great sadness and, I must say, that I cannot see any way by which it can be freed from it. The conduct of the ministry in general is not able to free them from it, nor the present dispensation of the word. It almost seems as if this carelessness is from the Lord and that he has the intention of leading the nation into judgment by it. And whether that judgment arrives in one way or in another, and even if we fail to discern its beginnings, we will certainly all be concerned in it. 'Who can endure the day of his coming?' (Mal. 3:2).

We would do well, brothers, to consider the state of the church of God in the world and among ourselves, and to consider our own condition. There seems to me, I must confess, to be a great decay in all the churches of Christ in the nation, especially among those of us who have had most peace and prosperity. That which we call zeal for God is almost completely lost among us. Some of us have almost forgotten whether there exists such a thing as the cause of Christ in the world. We, who once cried and prayed about it and had it upon our hearts, have sat down in our narrow compass and almost forgotten that there is such a thing as the interest of Christ in the world, inspiring us to an active zeal for the ordinances of God according to his rule, as God requires of us. Our first love? How decayed it is! The value of the ordinances of Christ and the fellowship of his people for our edification? How cold have we become to these things! How little is the church society upon our hearts, which some of us remember as being the very joy of our souls! Truly, we have reason to lift up our cry to God that he would return and visit the churches and pour out a new, fresh, reviving spirit upon them, so that we do not fall so much under the power of these decays that we become completely formal. God would then withdraw himself from us and leave us; which he seems to be at the very point of doing.

Finally, brothers, let us remember our own church: that God would, in a very special way, revive the spirit of life, power and holiness among us; that he would be pleased to help the officers of the church to discharge their duties and not allow them to fall under any declension of grace or gifts that would disqualify them from discharging their office for the good of the church; that he would keep them also from any lapse into formality in the exercise of their gifts of ministry; that he would take care of us, since we are so apt to fall in these ways. Let us pray that we may be acted upon by the Spirit of God and enlivened by the grace of God in everything that we do.

May the Lord help us to know the plague of our own hearts, and to be enabled to plead with him for grace and mercy to help us in every time of need.

4. Spiritual backsliding

Question: *How may we recover from spiritual backsliding?*

Answer: We have been talking of a decline in the principles of grace and I wish to offer a few thoughts that may help us recover from this declension. I will only be speaking of things that I have found helpful for myself.

If we are to recover spiritual life, we must come as near as we can to the source of that life, and remain there for as long as we are able. Christ is the spring of our spiritual life; he is in every way our life.

Before I describe how we should draw near and remain near to this wellspring of life, let me underline one thing. Men are careful about their health and safety at all times but whenever a general infectious disease arises (the plague, or something similar), everyone will be particularly watchful to avoid being infected by it. Now if departing from this spring of life is the prevalent plague of our age, and the plague of our locality, and the plague of Christians, we ought to be particularly careful that it does not reach us in some degree or other. It is quite clear to me that the apostasy, this cursed apostasy, that has spread itself over this country, with its fruits of ungodliness and uncleanness, consists of an apostasy and departure from the person of Christ. The authors of our day write of how little use the person of Christ is in religion; that his work was only that of bringing the gospel to us. Consider the preaching and moralising that we hear today. Most of it is preaching and discoursing about virtue and vice, just as in the days of the philosophers of old. But Jesus Christ is laid aside as if quite forgotten, as if he was of no use and of no consideration in religion, as if men did not know in what way he contributes to the living of a life near to God.

If we are wise we should consider very carefully whether we ourselves have been influenced by this apostasy. A general tendency can affect all men, even the best of believers, and prevail upon our spirits. I am afraid that some of us do not have that love for Christ, that delight in him, that we used to have, nor do we spend as much time with him as we once did. Jesus Christ, who is the life and centre, the glory and the power, of all spiritual life and of all that we have with respect to God, has been missing, to a considerable extent, from our faith and affections… But this is his commandment, 'Abide in me, and I in you. As the branch cannot bear fruit by itself, unless it abides in the vine, neither can you, unless you abide in me' (John 15:4).

'Well,' you ask, 'how are we to do this? How may we abide, more than we have done, near to this wellspring of life?' Here are four ways for us to do so:

(1) We are to abide at the source of all life by frequently acting in faith upon the person of Christ. Faith is not only that grace by which we were implanted into Christ, but also the grace by which we abide in him. Therefore, to act frequently in faith upon the person of Christ is to draw near to the source of life. Even though we might be vigorous, earnest and watchful of our hearts in our obedience, endeavouring to walk with God and to live for him, yet to fail to continue to act in faith upon Christ's person will weaken us, and we shall be the losers by it. Do you all understand me? I am not speaking just to the wisest and most knowledgeable of the flock but to the very least. I say that, even if we resolved with great earnestness, care and watchfulness, to fulfil our duties—even our inward duties of watching over our hearts—yet if by so doing we were kept from frequent acting in faith upon Christ, as the spring of our life, our spiritual life would decline. Therefore brothers, let me give you this advice, that you should, day and night, upon your beds, in your ways, on all occasions, exercise your faith on the person of Christ. Put your faith to work in viewing him as he is represented in the gospel, in trusting in him, and in praying to him—that he may be continually near to you. And you cannot have *him* near to *you* unless, by these acts of faith through grace, you make *yourselves* continually near to *him*. In this way you will abide at the wellspring.

(2) We are to abide in him in love. O, the warm affections for Christ which some of you can testify to: that your hearts were filled with love to Christ when you were under his call to believe in him! And to abide with Christ with love is a marvellous way of abiding in him. It is called cleaving to God and Christ (Acts 11:23). It is the affection of adhesion and gives a sense of union.

How then may we get our hearts to abide with Christ by love?

If I were to preach on this subject, how many things would offer themselves for consideration: the excellence of his person; the excellence of his love; our need of him; the advantages and benefits we have by him; his kindness towards us! All these things and many more, would quickly present themselves to us.

But I will only mention one thing, and mention it particularly because I heard it referred to in prayer a moment ago. Labour to have your hearts filled with love to Jesus Christ because in him is represented to us all that is excellent in God. This was God's glorious design. It is not to be separated from his design of glorifying himself in the work of redemption, because a large part of God's glorious design in the incarnation of Christ was to represent himself to us in Christ, 'who is the image of the invisible God, the express image of his person.'

If you were to consider Christ as God is gloriously represented to you in him, you would find him the most proper object for divine love—that love which is wrought in your hearts by the Holy Spirit—that love which has so much sweetness, complacency and satisfaction in it. Let us remember then to exercise our minds to consider Christ, in that all the lovely properties of the divine nature and all the counsels of God's will involving his love and grace, are manifested to us by Christ.

(3) We are to abide in him by adding meditation to our love and faith. Study more of Christ and of all the things of Christ. Delight more in hearing of Christ and in the preaching of Christ. He is your best friend; do not let the mysteries of his person and his grace deter you. There are wonderful things to do with the counsels of heaven and the glory of the holy God to be found in the person of Christ as the head of the church. If you study these things you will find an unsearchable treasure of divine wisdom, grace and love laid up in Jesus Christ. Let me assure you that this will prove the best expedient for the recovery of your spiritual life.

(4) Lastly, brothers, in that we are aware of a decline of spiritual life in the performance of our many duties, make every effort to bring spirituality into your duties.

'What is that?' you will say. 'What does it involve?'

It is the appropriate exercise of every grace that is required in order to discharge that duty. If every such grace is appropriately exercised, then the duty will be spiritually performed. For example, do you wish to be spiritual in your prayers? Then consider what graces are required for this duty: a proper fear and reverence of the name of God; faith, love and delight in him; a humble sense of your wants, earnest desires for supply, a dependence upon God for guidance, and so on. We all know that these are the graces required to fulfil this duty of praying by the Holy Spirit. Ensure that these graces are in evidence and you will then be spiritual in your prayers.

Is the duty that of charity, of giving to the poor? Then there should be a ready mind, a compassionate heart and obedience to Christ's command in this matter. These are the appropriate graces for this duty, and we must watch against any opposite feelings.

This is the way that we may bring spirituality into our duties: exercising the various graces appropriate for each duty.

I shall give just one more warning. Be careful that your head might not be so full of ideas and your tongue so fast to talk, that you empty your hearts of truth. We are prone to store up truth in our heads and talk about it often, and not let it affect our hearts, and this greatly weakens our spiritual life. The word preached among you, and the nature of what we preach, are great responsibilities upon us, because we must give an account of our preaching, and truly many a good word is preached. Yet we see such little fruit resulting. And the reason for this is that some, when they hear it, pay no further notice to it but 'drift away from it,' as the apostle describes it (Heb. 2:1). And if we complain of the weakness of our memories, this is just the easiest excuse for drifting away from the word. It is not the weakness of our memories that is at fault but the weakness of our hearts and affections, resulting in hearts that are like broken cisterns, hearts full of rents through which the water pours out, as Jeremiah depicts it (Jer. 2:13). The word slips out while we are putting our affections on worldly things, and it very quickly leaves that heart that gives it so little welcome. We talk away a sermon and the effect it had upon us; this robs us of the sermon and of its fruit. A man hears a good word of truth and, instead of taking the power of it into his heart, he takes the ideas of it into his mind and is satisfied with that. But this is not the way to thrive. God grant that we might never preach to you anything except that which we have first laboured to have felt the power of in our own hearts, and which we have first profited from ourselves! And may God grant also that you too may have some profit from the word ministered to you—that it might not slip out through worldly affections and that you might not drift away from it by ideas and talk, and have no regard for treasuring it up in your hearts!

We are to attend to these things diligently if we are to recover the spiritual losses of which we complain, and not without just cause.

5. Praying to Christ

Question: *Some have asked how it is we should pray to Jesus Christ; that is, how particularly are we to think of and apprehend the person of Christ as we pray to him?*

Answer: In that some judge that it is wrong to bring our worship to Christ as he is in his human nature, I shall share my thoughts and views on this.

(1) We must be careful that we have no conception of Christ, as we fulfil our duties towards him or relating to him, except in terms of his person as he is both God and man. It is not lawful for us to have any apprehension of

Christ, or to make any application to him, as man only. Nor is it lawful for us to have any apprehension of him as God only. All our apprehensions of Christ, and all our prayers to him, must be to him as God and man in one person. So he is, and so he will be to all eternity. The union is inseparable and indissoluble, and for any man to present a prayer to Christ either as God or as man, is to set up a false Christ. Christ is God and man in one person, and is nothing else. So, in all our acting in faith upon him and all our prayers to him, we should consider him as 'the seed of David' (Rom. 1:3) and as 'God over all, blessed for ever' (Rom. 9:5), in one person. This truth highlights the great idolatry of Roman Catholics: in their images of Christ they represent the human nature of Christ separated from his Deity. It is impossible for them to represent one that is God and man in one person, and so they become guilty of a double idolatry: conceiving of him as a man, and no more, and doing so by means of an image.

(2) The person of Christ is the immediate and proper object of all divine worship. His worship is commanded in the first commandment. By worship I mean faith, love, trust, submission of soul, and calling on his name—every act of the soul and mind by which we ascribe infinite, divine excellencies to God. This is the worship of the mind, John 5:23. It is the will of God 'that all may honour the Son, just as they honour the Father.' But how do we honour the Father? By divine faith, trust, love and worship. And so the Son must be honoured in the same way.

(3) The divine person of the Son of God lost nothing of the glory and honour that was due to him when he

assumed our human nature. Though he became the Son of Man in this way, as well as the Son of God—a Lamb for sacrifice—yet he is still, in his whole and entire person, the object of all that worship that I outlined above. The whole church of God agrees together in giving him that worship:

> And when he had taken the scroll, the four living creatures and the twenty-four elders fell down before the Lamb, each holding a harp, and golden bowls full of incense, which are the prayers of the saints. And they sang a new song, saying: 'Worthy are you to take the scroll and to open its seals, for you were slain, and by your blood you ransomed people for God from every tribe and language and people and nation...' Then I looked, and I heard around the throne and the living creatures and the elders the voice of many angels, numbering myriads of myriads and thousands of thousands, saying with a loud voice, 'Worthy is the Lamb who was slain, to receive power and wealth and wisdom and might and honour and glory and blessing!' And I heard every creature in heaven and on earth and under the earth and in the sea, and all that is in them, saying, 'To him who sits on the throne and to the Lamb be blessing and honour and glory and might for ever and ever!'—Rev. 5:8, 9, 11-13

Jesus Christ is here distinguished from the Father. We have 'him who sits on the throne' and also 'the Lamb' (where he is considered as incarnate, as 'the Lamb who was *slain*'). Yet, all the glory, honour, praise and worship that is given to him who sits on the throne, is also given to Jesus

Christ, God and man, the Lamb slain, who has redeemed us with his blood.

(4) This person of Christ, the God-man, must not be separated in any way by any conception of the mind. We may consider him, who is God and man, either, firstly, absolutely in himself, or, secondly, as he fulfils the office of Mediator. And this double consideration produces a double kind of worship of the person of Christ.

(a) When Christ is considered absolutely, in his own person, as the Son of God incarnate, he is the immediate and ultimate object of our faith, prayer and invocation. You may therefore lawfully, under the guidance and leading of the Holy Spirit, direct your prayers to the person of Christ. You have the example of Stephen in his last prayer. 'Lord Jesus,' he said, 'receive my spirit' (Acts 7:59). These were also the words of our Lord Jesus Christ when he died, 'Father, into your hands I commit my spirit!' (Luke 23:46). And Stephen, when he died, committed his spirit into the hands of Jesus Christ: 'Lord Jesus,' (for that is the name of the Son of God incarnate; 'You shall call his name Jesus, for he will save his people from their sins,' Matt. 1:21) 'receive my spirit.' A person therefore may make an immediate address in his prayers and supplications to the person of Christ, as God and man. I look upon it as the highest act of faith that a believer is called to in this world—to resign a departing soul into his hands, letting go all present things and future hopes; to resign a departing soul quietly and peaceably into the hands of Christ. This is what Stephen did with respect to Jesus. He left himself in Christ's hands in faith. Therefore we also may apply ourselves to him on any account and upon any occasion, in an act of faith.

(b) On the other hand, Christ may be considered as he discharges his mediatory office. And in this formal capacity, as mediator, he is not the ultimate object of our faith and invocation. Rather, we call upon God, the Father, in the name of Jesus Christ. We are those 'who through him [Christ] are believers in God' says Peter (1 Pet. 1:21). If this was not the case there would be a contradiction; the very name of mediator shows that he is the means by which we approach God. It would be a contradiction to say that our faith terminated on him in his mediatory office. Christ calls this, 'asking the Father in his name,' as, for example, in, 'whatever you ask the Father in my name' (John 15:16). That is, he tells us to plead specifically the intervention of his mediation. This is also what the apostle tells us in his great rubric and directory of church worship, 'For through him we both have access in one Spirit to the Father' (Eph. 2:18). The Father is placed before us as the ultimate object of access in our worship; the Spirit is the effecting cause, enabling us in this worship; the Son is the means by which we approach to God.

All that I shall add to this is the following: Seeing that there is in Scripture this double worship of Christ (as he is absolutely, and as he is as Mediator between God and man) which of these ought we principally to engage in?

Let me answer plainly:

(i) The Scriptures generally point us, for solemn worship in the church, towards Christ as Mediator. The general worship that is to be performed to God in the assemblies of the saints considers Christ as executing his mediatory office, and so our address is to the throne of grace by him. By him we enter into the holy place—through him and by him to God. 'I bow my knees unto the Father of our Lord Jesus Christ' (Eph. 3:14). God, considered as the Father of our Lord Jesus Christ, is the proper ultimate object of the solemn worship of the church.

(ii) In treating and dealing with respect to our own souls, as the Spirit of God leads us, it is lawful and expedient for us in our prayers and supplications to address the person of Christ, as Stephen did.

6. Applying to Christ for grace

Question: *How are we to pray to Christ for increased grace; that is, that we may have our grace strengthened and ready for all exercise? Or, how should we pray to Christ that we might receive grace from him so that we recover from backsliding?*

Answer: I think that the direction given by our Saviour himself is so plain, and so fitted to our experience, that we do not need to look much further. He says, 'As the branch cannot bear fruit by itself, unless it abides in the vine, neither can you, unless you abide in me' (John 15:4). What we aim for is fruit-bearing, which consists just as much in the internal vigorous actions of grace as in the performances of outward duties; to be faithful in our minds and souls as well as in our lives. 'The way to do that,' says the Saviour, 'is to abide in me' (John 15:4). And he tells us plainly that, unless we do so, whatever else we will do, we cannot bear fruit. So then the whole of our fruitfulness depends on our abiding in Christ.

Not much more, therefore, can be said of this question, except to look a little into what abiding in Christ means.

It is certainly not merely a not-going-away from Jesus, in the sense that we say that someone abides when they are not moving away. For I hope that for all the decays that we complain of and the want of fruitfulness, we have not yet left Christ and gone away from him. We still abide in him in the sense that the branch abides in the root, from where it receives its communication and supplies. Therefore there is something specific meant by this abiding in Christ, this dwelling in Christ and Christ dwelling in us.

There seems to be the following involved: that to abide in Christ is to be always near to Christ, in the spiritual company of Christ, and in communication with Christ. It does not lie in the pure, essential act of believing, by which we are implanted into Christ and cannot be parted from him; but there is rather something of a special, spiritual activity of the soul in this abiding in Christ. It is an abiding in him and in his presence.

As this abiding in Christ is achieved by certain actions of our souls, then let us consider what kind of acts these may be in order to gain some more light on the matter. They must certainly involve actions of the mind, of the will and of the affections.

Firstly, there is an abiding with Christ by the use of our minds. This involves contemplation and thoughts of him, night and day. 'On my bed by night I sought him whom my soul loves' says the spouse (Song of Sol. 3:1). We are to consider often the person of Christ, to think of him as invested in his glorious office and entrusted and designed by the Father for this work. 'We all,' says the apostle, 'with unveiled face, beholding the glory of the Lord, are being transformed into the same image from one degree of glory to another. For this comes from the Lord who is the Spirit' (2 Cor. 3:18).

Brothers, what you and I are aiming at is to be 'transformed into the same image,' that is, into the image and likeness of the glory of God in Christ. I am bold enough to say, for those of us who have been brought to have a daily sense of leaving this world and the present state of things, that we have no greater longing than that we might be more and more changed into that image before we go out of this world. There is nothing that we look for more often than our perfection in likeness to Christ. Therefore older Christians especially will bear witness that we long, more than anything, to be more and more changed into Christ's likeness. How shall we get to this? 'Why,' says the apostle, 'by looking steadily at Christ, just as a man looks at a far away object with a telescope. We behold him by looking steadily at Christ himself, and the glory of God in him.' And there is a wonderfully large object for us to look at, for when you look at the glory of God in Christ you have the whole of Christ to view: the person of Christ; the office of Christ; the merit of Christ; the example of Christ; the death of Christ, and whatever you wish, as long as your thoughts are full of Christ. I do not know how you find things, brothers, but the advice that I would give to older Christians, who are not likely to continue long in this world, is to exercise yourselves in immediate contemplations of

Christ. The main purpose of all the teaching that you have received from ministers has been to enable you to do this. Truly, if I know anything, we shall find such thoughts to be accompanied by a sweet transforming power greater than anything we have experienced in other ways and duties. We shall be 'transformed into the same image.'

We abide in Christ therefore in the acts of our minds by our thoughts and meditations of Christ in the night and upon our beds, in our walks and by the wayside, and in times set aside for meditation. We are to work hard for an intuitive view of Christ; that is, a clear view of him in our thoughts.

Secondly, if you are to abide in Christ, there must be an acting of your will involved also: proceeding with great diligence and carefulness with respect to every act of obedience that Christ requires of us. To work hard at having wills that are ready to perform every act of obedience that Christ requires at our hands is a very large part of abiding in him. Let this question be always in our minds whether any action on our part is God's will, or not. If it is so, let us be ready to show that we are abiding in Christ by yielding cheerful and willing obedience to him in it. We should every one of us think often of this: what is it that Christ requires of me personally in any way of duty and obedience? We should be especially ready to recognize that Christ requires us to live very circumspectly and carefully—to keep ourselves from the pollutions and defilements that arise by our converse in the world. Christ requires this at all times, in all instances and on all occasions. What do we teach? And what have all your former teachers been instructing you? That you should know all the duties, and the steps to fulfil them, that Christ requires from you. And 'if you know these things, blessed are you if you do them' (John 13:17).

This is your fruit-bearing: a direct contemplation of Christ (and you will find that Christ will draw nearer to you and visit your heart more frequently when you keep this duty than he does for any other); to have our hearts ready to comply with every instance of obedience that he requires.

Thirdly, there is an abiding in Christ with respect to our affections. There may be love and delight involved in all the actions described above. Indeed, if there is not, very little spiritual benefit will result. There is no duty required of any man in this world, however spiritual or heavenly or evangelical it may be, but that, for lack of love and delight, a man may be lazy in fulfilling it. I may tie myself to perform this or that duty for this or that hour, yet have no benefit to my own soul, nor give any glory to God, if there is no love and delight in it. These sweeten the duty and refresh the heart of God and man, Christ and us. Labour therefore, brothers, and pray, that you may abide in Christ with delight; that you may find a sweetness and refreshment in so doing; that every time of turning to Christ may bring a spiritual joy and gladness to your heart. Now is a great opportunity, shaking off all the distractions of life and other concerns, to dwell with Christ. Now is a good time.

7. Weak faith when praying

Question: *At times we have very little faith that our prayers will be heard. We are hindered by unbelief from expecting an answer and we feel we have no grounds for being heard. What are the factors at work in us at such times making our faith so weak?*

Answer: If our hearts have not been prepared beforehand and affected by considering the great and glorious properties, presence and holiness of God, then certainly we will lack the faith to believe that our prayers will be answered. It is also of great importance that we have a correct view of the context in which the things for which we pray are promised to us: whether they are temporal things, which are dependent on God's will; or spiritual things that are promised, so that we may press God immediately about them.

There are two things that weaken our faith as to whether our prayers will be answered.

The first is that mixture of self which is apt to creep into our prayers, especially in our public prayers in the congregation and assemblies. An awareness of our own reputation as we exercise our gifts will certainly weaken faith.

The second is a proneness to pray earnestly and fervently, with noisy, high-sounding speech, but with no diligent pursuing of the things for which we pray. Unless we watch out for and follow after these things we shall have no foundation for a faith that the prayers will be answered. Thus, for example, our soul might be burdened by some personal sin and we may be at our most fervent in praying to God against it. Yet, having done this, if we are not particularly careful in ensuring that we mortify that sin, where is there any faith in us that our prayer will be answered? We must pursue our prayers or our faith will be weakened. We all pray, but do we believe that God will hear and answer our prayers?

I do not intend to speak on the nature of faith, or on the assurance we have of the answering of our prayers, but to tell you plainly of those factors within ourselves that hinder this.

(1) We are not clear on that great truth that our persons are accepted. God had respect to Abel and his offering and not to Cain and his offering. We cannot have more faith that our prayers are heard than we have that our persons are accepted. How many of us doubt and do not know whether we truly believe or not? Or whether we are the children of God or not? According to our faith that we are personally accepted so, in general, will be our faith as to the hearing of our prayers. I acknowledge that sometimes, under extraordinary darkness or temptation, when a person does not know at all or have any assurance as to his own position before God, yet the Holy Spirit may give an assurance that a prayer poured out in anguish of soul has been heard. But, in general, let us not complain that our prayers are not being heard when we ourselves are still negligent in seeking assurance of the real condition of our souls before God. We may have had many days of prayer and still not experienced that return of prayer that we hoped for. And at the root of the matter lies this evil: that we doubt our position before God. Labour, first of all, to amend such a state of affairs.

(2) Another thing is this: however much you pray you will not believe that your prayers will be answered if you are indulging any private sin, or not vigorously attempting to mortify it, as the Scriptures and duty require. If any lust rises in the soul and we do not immediately make every effort to mortify it, as God requires, it will break out and weaken our faith in all our prayers. Therefore, if you wish for stronger faith in prayer, make sure you search your heart. Do not believe that only those sins that break out into open sin are those you indulge. It may be that you have not discerned every corruption that you indulge. Work hard therefore to find out what you have missed, and you will then discover how it is weakening your faith.

(3) Again, another factor is the lack of treasuring up former experiences of the answering of prayer. We have not gathered our stores as we should have in this matter. If we had laid up various experiences of God hearing and answering our prayers it would strengthen our faith that he will do so again. It may be that some have prayed all their lives; through all the years God has kept their souls; they have not wickedly departed from God; they have obtained specific mercies. Such believers ought to keep a constant record of these divine answers to their prayers. Every discovery made of Christ that brings our souls closer to him and increases our love to him, is an experience of God answering our prayers.

(4) I might add a last factor which is an awareness that our prayers have lost that fervency which should be typical of those who believe. When we pray in the congregation,

on our own or in the family and, having finished, are aware that we have not interceded with appropriate urgency then, at such times, we cannot believe that such prayers will be heard.

It is the duty of all men to pray to the Lord; but it is the particular responsibility of those who have really and truly given themselves to God but have no comfortable assurance that this is the case. Far from discouraging those in such a situation from praying, I would argue that this is the period in your life when you are most called to prayer. When Paul was first called, before he had any evidence of the pardon of his sins, it was said of him, 'Behold, he is praying' (Acts 9:11). If those uncertain of their condition were aware of the seriousness of their position it would certainly be said of them, like Paul, 'Behold, they pray.' And even in these prayers, they exercise faith, even when they themselves cannot find the faith in themselves to believe in an answer.

8. Prevailing sins

Question: *When should any one particular sin, lust or corruption, be considered a habitual sin, one which has taken root within us?*

Answer: I shall consider some general matters before addressing the question directly.

First of all, all sins and lusts of whatever kind have their root and residence in our nature, even the very worst of them. For, as the apostle James says, 'Each person is tempted when he is lured and enticed by his own desire' (James

1:14). Every man has his own lust and every man has all lust in him, for this lust or desire is the depravity of our nature, and is in all men. And the root and principle of it remains in men even after they have been converted. As Paul says of believers, 'The desires of the flesh are against the Spirit... to keep you from doing the things you want to do' (Gal. 5:17). What does the flesh desire to do? The works of the flesh, namely 'sexual immorality, impurity, sensuality, idolatry, sorcery, enmity, strife, jealousy, fits of anger, rivalries, dissensions, divisions, envy, drunkenness, orgies, and things like these' (Gal. 5:19-21). The flesh desires all these things in believers, the worst things that can be mentioned.

This is the reason for that teaching of our Saviour when he foresaw profound troubles, great desolations and destructions coming upon the earth and afflicting all men, describing that day as 'coming upon you suddenly like a trap. For it will come upon all who dwell on the face of the whole earth' (Luke 21:34, 35). Nothing makes me believe more that that day, that terrible day of the Lord, is coming, than this description of it as coming like a trap, a snare. The Saviour says that men take no notice of this, but as for us: 'Watch yourselves lest your hearts be weighed down with dissipation and drunkenness and cares of this life, and that day come upon you suddenly' (Luke 21:34). What we learn from this is that, at the approach of the worst of times, the best of men need to be warned to be watchful against the worst of sins. Who would think that when such troubles and distresses were coming upon a nation,

Christ's disciples should be in danger of being overtaken by dissipation and drunkenness and the cares of this life? Yet he, who is the wisdom of God, knew how we would behave. We might even say from our own observation that believers are never in more danger of sensual, provoking sins than when destruction is lying nearest at the door. 'In that day,' he says, 'watch yourselves.'

Secondly, notice that this root of sin dwelling within us will, if it has opportunity, work itself out into all sorts of evil. This should give us a godly jealousy over our souls and over one another. 'Sin... produced in me all kinds of covetousness,' says the apostle (Rom. 7:8).

Thirdly, because sin always dwells in us and will, on occasion, produce its fruit in all kinds of covetousness, then the mortification of sin is a continual duty in which we should be engaged every day of our lives. 'You have died, and your life is hidden with Christ in God' (Col. 3:3). What a blessed state and condition! I do not wish for any better ambition in the world than that which this offers. But notice the duty that the apostle infers from it. 'Therefore,' he says, 'Put to death what is earthly in you' (Col 3:5). And what is that? 'Sexual immorality, impurity, passion, evil desire and covetousness, which is idolatry.' The mortification of sin is a duty required from the best of saints.

Fourthly, any particular sin does not become a habitual, ever-present sin, unless it is given some particular advantage. Our corrupt nature is universally and indiscriminately corrupt, but a particular sin becomes pre-eminent by being given particular advantages.

It would be too long to speak of all these advantages. I shall consider two of them, which cover all possibilities, in general.

(1) The inclinations of our constitution will give particular advantages to some particular sins. Some men may be very much inclined to envy, some to wrath and passion, others to sensual sins—gluttony, drunkenness, uncleanness (to name those that our Saviour warns us of). It is with respect to these that some think David referred when he said that he will keep himself from his guilt (Psa. 18:23). I can only say this: that men who plead their temperaments and the inclinations of their constitutions to extenuate their sins, are woefully deceived by the lies of the devil. Rather, their situation only aggravates their guilt. 'I am apt to be passionate by nature,' says one; 'I am very sociable,' says another, 'and love company.' They make their natural constitution to be a cover and excuse for their sin. But in my judgment, I believe that if grace does not cure constitution-sins, it cures none, and that we have nothing to trial and test the efficacy of grace if it does not cure constitution-sins. The great promise is that grace will change the nature of the wolf, the lion, the bear, the cobra and the adder, and that they shall become like lambs. This it will never achieve unless it does so by a continual counterworking of the inclinations that arise from our constitutions.

(2) Our outward circumstances will give particular advantage to some sins. These may be considered under two headings:

(a) Education. Particular sins take advantage of our education and upbringing. If, by education, by fine clothes and by the behaviour we require of them, we instruct our children in pride, we heap dry fuel upon them, until such time as lust will flare up. Let us beware of this. It is an easy thing to bring forth a proud generation in this way.

(b) The society around us. The society in which we find ourselves according to our circumstances in life can inflame particular corruptions. To the degree that men delight in the world's society so sins will be provoked and heightened by it.

Having spoken of the nature of this danger, and how it arises, let me address the question directly: How may we know if a particular sin has become habitually predominant within us?

Brothers, I take it for granted that the vilest of those sins which our Saviour and his apostles warned us against, commanded that we should mortify and crucify them, may be working in the hearts and minds of the best of us. And also, that a particular sin may be our besetting sin even though, for various reasons, it may not manifest evident outward effects. Therefore, be warned.

Firstly, note that when the mind and soul is frequently and strongly urged upon and pressed with a particular lust and corruption, this does not mean that that particular sin has taken root in the heart. This may be purely temptation. It may all proceed from the conjunction of a particular temptation with indwelling sin. This may then result in fighting and warring, in the using of force and, sometimes, in defeat and subsequent sinning.

But suppose a person is in this situation, how can he know whether his experience is a result of a particular temptation coinciding with indwelling sin, or whether this is the habitual action of a particular, prevailing, deep-rooted sin? I answer:

1. It is not a habitual sin in the three following cases:

(a) When the soul is grieved by it more than it is defiled by it. In this case, it is a temptation and not a habitually present lust. When a heart is enticed by a sin, sin and grace are both at work, having opposite aims. The aim of grace is to humble the heart and the aim of sin is to defile it. And the soul is defiled if, by the deceitfulness and solicitations of sin, consent is obtained. The defilement arises, not from the temptation as it is active in the mind but from the temptation as it is admitted with consent. To the degree in which the soul consents, whether after being taken by surprise or after long struggles, to that extent it is defiled. But there is no rooted sin here if the soul is more grieved and troubled by the temptation than defiled by it.

(b) When the soul truly views that particular corruption as its greatest and mortal enemy. 'It is not soldiers that have ruined my estate, nor a disease that has taken away my health, nor enemies who have ruined my name or opposed me, but this corruption, which is my great and mortal enemy.' When this is the true feeling of the soul, then it is to be hoped that it is under the power of a temptation and not in the grip of a habitual sin.

(c) Also, when a man wars and struggles against the corruption constantly, especially in the two great duties of private prayer and meditation. If the soul is stopped from these, it will be driven off the field, and sin is the conqueror. But so long as a man maintains the conflict by the exercise of these gracious duties, I judge that the case is one of temptation and not a habitual, prevalent lust.

(2) What, therefore, are the evidences of a prevailing sin? This is a large topic, but I shall only mention a few things:

(a) When a man willingly and knowingly embraces opportunities to indulge in his sin, that sin is habitually present. Everyone who has the general understanding of a Christian and who has a corruption or lust working within him knows the circumstances that provoke it. No man, unless he is profligately wicked, will choose sin for sin's sake, but anyone who knows the situations that stir up, excite, and draw forth, any particular sin, and chooses them, or willingly embraces them, is guilty of harbouring a habitual sin to a high degree. All such occasions for a particular sin must be avoided otherwise its power will never be defeated.

(b) When anyone finds that the arguments against a particular sin are losing their force, they should fear that that sin has become prevalent. Anyone vulnerable to a particular corruption knows the arguments drawn from fear, danger, shame and ruin, against continuing in that sin. But if these arguments should begin to appear less powerful, and to arise more infrequently in his mind, then let that man realise that his sin is rooted within him.

(c) There is habitual sin present when a man, though forced to turn aside from continuing in it, yet is not turned away from his purpose. He pursues his way like the wild donkey, 'in her heat sniffing the wind' (Jer. 2:24). If you meet her or overtake her you may turn her out of her way, but still she pursues her design. Men may meet with strong convictions of sin, strong rebukes and reproofs, and these may cause them to hesitate a little, but do not weaken their purpose and inclination. The bent of their spirit still lies in the same direction and the secret language of their heart is still, 'that it were free with me to be as in former days!' A sin is certainly prevalent if it seldom or never fails to act when given the opportunity. If a trader cheats every time he is able to, he has covetousness in his heart; if, whenever an opportunity to drink arises, a man does so to excess, that is proof of a prevailing habit; very rarely is he able to resist whenever temptation and opportunity coincide.

(d) A prevailing sin is present when the soul, on self-examination, will find that it has lost all evidence of renewing grace and is, at best, only under the influence of restraining grace. Believers are acted upon by renewing grace; yet there are occasions when under the power of corruption and temptation they rebel against this rule. God then keeps them in order by restraining grace: by the fear of danger, shame and infamy. These outward considerations, brought home forcibly to the mind by the Holy Spirit, keep them from sinning. But if a man finds that his heart has completely freed itself from the rule of renewing grace and that nothing tempers his behaviour apart from restraining grace, then his sin has gained a complete victory over him; that is, he would sin on to the end of his life, were it not for fear of shame, danger, death and hell. He is no longer acted upon by renewing grace—faith working by love. Any man who has spiritual understanding may examine himself and discover what exactly is his state and what it is that rules his heart.

(e) Lastly, when sinning is the predominant inclination of the will, then lust is habitually prevalent. Sin may entangle the mind or disorder the affections, and still not be prevalent. But once it has gained hold of the will, it has the mastery.

9. Can habitual sin coexist with grace?

Question: *Is lust or corruption, when habitually prevalent, consistent with the presence of grace?*

Answer: This is a hard question. There are difficulties with it, and it may be that it cannot be answered precisely. We have to be particularly careful as to how we answer it; it is a question that determines the present and eternal condition of men's souls.

Let us remember what was considered in the previous discussion with respect to a prevalent lust or sin, because that will be the basis of our answer to the present question.

Firstly, it is the duty of every believer to take care that this should never be true of him in practice. We shall meet with enough difficulties and enough doubts and fears about our eternal condition even if we have no prevailing sin or corruption. It is, therefore, the duty of every believer to take care that this should never happen to him or her. This is what David did, 'Who can discern his errors?' he says. 'Keep back your servant also from presumptuous sins; let them not have dominion over me' (Psa. 19:12, 13). He acknowledges his errors and sins, and prays for cleansing, purifying pardon. But for presumptuous sins, sins indulged with a high hand, and every habitual corruption that has something of presumption in it, he prays, 'LORD, keep back your servant from them' (Psa. 19:13). We see the same caution in the apostle's letter to the Hebrews, 'See to it that no one fails to obtain the grace of God; that "no root of bitterness" springs up and causes trouble' (Heb. 12:15). There is a root of bitterness in everyone. I take this to mean a sin which is to some degree habitual, and has the potential to spring up and cause great defilement. I plead with you, brothers, for your own sakes and for mine, beg of God that we might be careful that this should never be true of us.

Secondly, whatever may be said of the consistency of a prevailing sin with the presence of grace, it is certainly inconsistent with the presence of peace. Let me ask you again to remember what was said previously about such sins, as we now consider the application of those words. Here (although I would wish, in treating the subject, to be as tender as if dealing with the apple of my eye) I will not fear to say that the peace felt by anyone in whom there is a prevailing sin, is only a sense of security and not a true peace.

I know that men while still under deep-rooted sins may be at great peace and live on good hopes that they will be accepted by God; that it shall be well with them at their last end; that they will have the strength at some time or other to strive against this corruption and overcome it. But all such peace is just a sense of security. Whenever such a sin is present there will always be a drawing back. I would explain it as follows: a person who professes faith and has kept up with his Christian duties and obedience but then, because of his constitution, his temptations or his walk of life, has fallen under the grip of some lust which has taken him away from his former walk with God, has drawn back. Now, says the apostle, 'If he shrinks back, my soul has no pleasure in him' (Heb. 10:38). And when God has no pleasure, whatever the degree of backsliding involved (it may, of course, even be that of final apostasy), he will not give any grounds from which that soul might derive peace. Likewise, in Isaiah 57:17, 'Because of the iniquity of his unjust gain I was angry... I hid my face and was angry.' If there is an incurable iniquity of covetousness or any other sin in us, whether active or not, God is angry and hides himself from us. I pray, brothers, let us examine our peace, and if we find that we have a peace that is able to hold its ground and station even when we harbour an abiding sin, let us not trust that peace any more. It will not stand us in good stead when we come to trial.

Thirdly, if a habitual sin is not inconsistent with true grace in the heart, it is certainly inconsistent with the true exercise of grace. It is not, indeed, inconsistent with the performance of duties but it is inconsistent with the true exercise of grace in the performance of those duties. It is often seen and appreciated that persons under prevalent corruptions will multiply duties, hoping to quieten their consciences and to compensate God for their sins. People may multiply prayers, follow preaching, and attend to other duties when, through the deceitfulness of sin, they are only using all these things as a cloak for some prevailing sin, and in all these duties there is no exercising of grace whatsoever.

A right understanding of this question depends on a right understanding of 1 John 2:15. If we could understand that verse it would determine the point for us. 'Do not love the world or the things in the world. If anyone loves the world, the love of the Father is not in him.' This verse addresses the question we are considering. I know that one exegesis of the verse is to the effect: 'If any man makes the world his chief good, if any man puts the world in the place of God, then the love of the Father is not in him; that is, either he has received no love from the Father, or he has no love for God as a Father in Christ.' But the apostle is addressing believers in this verse, and therefore I do not think that he is speaking in absolute terms but in matters of degree; that is, if love of the world is prevailing, there is no prevailing acting of love towards the Father. The verses do not speak of a constant principle of love to the world, or love to the Father, but of the prevailing action of the one or the other. Accordingly it may be said of all the other graces, that where the actions of sin prevail there is a suspension of the exercising of grace. Brothers, if any of us have been under the power of prevailing corruption (I will still speak gently, and of what ought to be received and believed, whether people are actually doing so or not), it is greatly to be feared that we have wasted all our praying and sermon-hearing, because we have not had a true exercise of grace in them. There may be some kind of exercise involved, but a true and appropriate exercise of grace will have been put to sleep by the continuing sin. Therefore let us be watchful of prevailing sin lest all our Christian works (our prayers, hearing of sermons, suffering, charity) be lost to us because of a lack of the exercise of grace in them.

Fourthly, I accept that spiritual life may be unconscious when the spiritual man is not dead. There is a kind of failure of the vital powers of the spirit—a fainting away—that may happen to believers, suspending all spiritual life, though the spiritual man is not dead. Therefore, though I might see all the evidences of the spiritual life of a man as being unconscious through the prevalence of sin, yet I would not immediately conclude that the spiritual man was dead. Take the case of David in the period between his great fall and the coming of Nathan the prophet. His fall, as one has described it, beat the breath out of his body and for a long time he lay like a dead man because of the power of that one crucial sin remaining in him. This may be taken as a powerful example of how one sin, not immediately mortified by due humility, may leave a great, even a continual tendency in the soul to that same sin. This is so much the case that some have seen it as the reason for the corruption of our nature. It is a difficult question in theology to explain how one particular sin, like Adam's sin, should bring habitual corruption into our nature. And some answer the question in this way: that any one single immoral act, carried out with a high hand, brings with it such an assault on rectitude as to dispose our whole nature to corruption. By that single act of flagrant wickedness, David's spiritual life fell away for this long period, until Nathan came and ministered good to him so as to recover him from his faint. Therefore I would not judge a person whom I have previously believed to possess spiritual life to be spiritually dead, though presently I see him seemingly bereft of all evidences of spiritual life. And the reason why I would so judge is this: because if you judge a person dead, you neglect him and leave him. But if you judge him to be in a spiritual faint, though this is such a dangerous state, yet you will use all possible means to retrieve his life. So ought we to do to one another and to our own souls.

Fifthly, there is, on the other hand, a complete prevailing of sin that is inconsistent with true grace and which may befall those who have been professors of faith. The apostle speaks of this clearly, 'Do you not know that if you present yourselves to anyone as obedient slaves, you are slaves of the one you obey, either of sin, which leads to death, or of obedience, which leads to righteousness?' (Rom. 6:16). There may be such a strong service of sin that it puts a man into a state opposite to that which he once professed.

Sixthly, there may be a corruption, or sin, or lust that is habitually present, by whatever evidences that person, or others, may discern, and yet the root of the matter, the root of spiritual life, may, notwithstanding, be in him.

How then, for such a man, do you suppose we might judge whether the root of the matter is in him?

If the soul has anything of spiritual life left in it there will be something of vital spiritual action within it. The two vital operations that evidence the soul is not completely slain by prevalent sin are opposition and humiliation. So long as the soul, however much it may be captivated, is conscious of the sincerity of its opposition to that sin, there is evidence of a vital life. And the same is the conclusion when it is constant in its humiliation for that sin.

It may further be asked, how may it be known that this humiliation is sincere?

It cannot be known by its vigour and efficacy, for these would make all such questioning unnecessary. If the opposition were vigorous and effectual it would break the power of the lust and corruption so that it is no longer prevalent. But there are two ways in which it may be known.

(a) By its constancy. If the root of the matter is still in us there will be a constant opposition to every act of any prevailing sin whatsoever. I am not talking about violent temptations but ordinary occasions. If a man does not sincerely oppose every instance of the acting of prevalent sin I do not see how we can conclude that there is spiritual life in him. If he can pass over one act and then another without a sense of humiliation in him, the holy, sovereign God show him grace and mercy! But to me, this is 'the way of a serpent on a rock' (Prov. 30:19). There is no evidence there to be seen!

(b) By its sincerity. If it is sincere it rises from a true source. That is, if the opposition to the sin does not arise only from conviction, or light, or conscience, but from the will of the poor sinner. 'I would do otherwise; I would that this sin might be destroyed. I would have it rooted out that it should no longer be in me. My will is against it, though it has captured my affections and taken me out of the way.'

The following is all that I dare to say on this question: there may be spiritual life in one in whom a prevalent sin abides, a sin of which he and others may be aware. We may discern the root of the matter in him by the actions of his spiritual life—his opposition to the sin beforehand, and his humiliation for it afterwards. We may know the sincerity of these vital actions by their constancy, and by their source—by our perseverance in them, and by their arising from our wills.

10. How may we be delivered from a habit of sin?

Question: *What should a person, who finds himself under the power of a prevailing sin or temptation, do?*

Answer: There are many degrees of prevailing sin. It may be a temptation that results in outward scandal, or in the utter loss of inward peace, or in the disturbance of that tranquillity of mind which Christ usually calls us to. My answer will apply to all these, to all degrees of this condition. All of us possibly have experienced at one time or another, to some degree or other, disturbance, loss of peace, or outward scandal.

What should a person do who finds himself in this state?

Firstly, he should make every effort to impress his mind with the danger of it. It is almost inconceivable how subtle sin is in distracting us from an apprehension of its danger. 'Notwithstanding this sin,' says a man, 'I still hope that I am in a state of grace, and shall be saved, and shall arrive in heaven eventually.' In this way the mind is distracted from a proper sense of danger. I beseech you, brothers and sisters, if this is true of you, make every effort to convince yourselves that being in such a state, as far as I know, will end in hell. Do not let your minds be turned away from the realisation that, on good grounds of faith, such ways will end in those paths that descend to the chambers of death. Do not please yourselves by imagining that you are members of the church and have good hopes of salvation by Jesus Christ, but consider where it is that such a course will take you, and impress this on your mind.

Secondly, when a person is affected with the danger of this condition, the next thing to be done is to burden the conscience with the guilt of it. For, just as our minds are slow to apprehend the danger, so also our consciences are very unwilling to take the weight of the burden of their guilt. I am not speaking of men with seared consciences; these, whatever the weight you put upon them, will feel nothing. But even the consciences of renewed men, unless they use all the ways and means by which consciences are burdened—by apprehensions of the holiness of God, of the law, of the love of Christ, and of all those things by which the conscience is to be made to feel the weight of its guilt—are slow to do this. No sooner does the conscience begin to feel a bit sick with a sense of the guilt of sin but it quickly finds a convenient remedy. 'I have committed this sin and contracted this and that guilt; I have long been negligent in this or that duty; I have long been engaged in this or that folly, and been so given up to the world. I must go to Christ by faith, or I am lost.' The conscience is afraid of measuring and feeling its load. Rather, let your conscience bear the burden and not shift it off so easily, unless it can by true faith, guided by the word, load it upon Christ. This is not something to be done negligently and lightly.

Thirdly, what should we do when we have this apprehension of our danger and are thus burdened with its guilt? Pray for deliverance. 'How,' you will say. In the Scriptures there is mention of 'roaring': 'The voice of my roaring' (Psa. 32:3); and similarly of 'shouting': 'I shouted and cried' (Lam. 3:8). This is a time to pray that God would not hide his face from our roaring nor shut out our prayers when we shout to him, that is, when we cry out with all the vigour of our souls. Christ is able to help those who cry to him (Heb. 2:18) and the word 'help' here refers to someone running to help a man who is about to be destroyed. These may seem hard things to us, but it is a great thing to save our soul and to deliver ourselves from the snares of Satan.

Fourthly, treasure up every warning and every word that you are convinced was aimed at your particular corruption. To everyone who is under the power of a particular corruption, God, at some time or other, by his providence or by his word, will give particular warnings, so that your soul may say: 'This is for me. I must comply with it.' But very often we respond like that man who looked in a mirror: 'He looks at himself and goes away and at once forgets what he was like' (James 1:23, 24); and there the matter ends. But if God gives you such warnings, note them down, treasure them up, do not lose them. They must be accounted for. 'He who is often reproved, yet stiffens his neck, will suddenly be broken beyond healing' (Prov. 29:1).

Fifthly, I would remind you of two rules and then conclude.

(1) In the midst of all your perplexities with respect to the power of sin, exercise faith, so that, notwithstanding all that you experience of being almost lost and gone, you will realise that there is a power in God, through Christ, for subduing and conquering it.

(2) It is in vain for anyone to think of mortifying a prevailing sin, who does not at the same time endeavour to mortify *all* sin. Consider a man who is troubled and perplexed with a particular temptation. He cries, 'O that I might be delivered! I would rather have deliverance than life! I will do my utmost to watch against it.' But it may be that this same man will not be constant in secret prayer. He might strive and fight and wish himself free from that sin, but he will not persist in those duties by which that lust must be mortified. Therefore, always remember this rule: never hope to mortify any corruption by which you are grieved in heart unless you strive to mortify every sin by which the Spirit of God is grieved, and unless you are found in every duty, especially those by which grace thrives and flourishes.

11. Days of judgment

Question: *What is our duty when undergoing dark and difficult experiences of God's providence in the world?*

Answer: There are three things to be considered when answering this question. Firstly, in a Scriptural sense, what is it that makes any particular providence a dark and difficult one? Secondly, what are the evident signs of the approach and departure of such a season? And thirdly, what are our special duties with respect to entering into and passing through such a season?

Firstly, there are four things in Scripture that define a dark season of providence and, unless I am mistaken, they are all upon us, presently.

(1) The long-continued prosperity of wicked men. You know that this is so often mentioned in the Old Testament: Psa.73; Jer. 12:1-3; Hab. 1:4, 13 and many other places. Holy men of old confessed themselves as being in great perplexity at the long-continued prosperity of wicked men, and their long-continued prosperity in the ways of wickedness. And if you add this further circumstance: the long-continued prosperity of wicked men in their wickedness when the light shines round about them to convince them of that wickedness; when God speaks in and by the light of his word against them—that is a great trial. When all things are wrapped up in darkness and idolatry, we do not wonder so much at the patience of God, but when matters arrive at such a state that many continue to prosper in wickedness even when their judgment is proclaimed to them—that is a difficult providence.

(2) It is a difficult season of providence when the church continues under persecution and distress even at a time when they have given themselves to prayer. This is the difficulty that seems to be mentioned in Psalm 80:4: 'O LORD God of hosts, how long will you be angry with your people's prayers?' This made it hard, that God should afflict

his church and keep her under distresses, suffer the furrows to be made long upon her back and continue her under oppression from one season to another. There may be very clear reasons for this at any time. But God has also said: 'Call upon me in the day of trouble; I will deliver you,' (Psa. 50:15). God has promised to avenge the church. 'Will not God give justice to his elect, who cry to him day and night?' (Luke 18:7). He will do it speedily. Now when he seems to be angry with the prayers of his people, that is a difficult season; when they cry and shout and God shuts out their prayers, that is a dark providence.

Just as the first difficulty is evidently upon us so also we have this other to contend with, that the anger of God continues to smoke against the prayers of his people. I hope that this is the case, for, having stirred up many a blessed cry to himself, there will be a time when he will hear and answer their prayers.

(3) It is a dark and difficult dispensation of providence when the world and the nations of the world are filled with confusion and blood, with no just reason appearing why it should be so. When our Saviour foretold a difficult season, he said, 'Nation will rise against nation, and kingdom against kingdom, and there will be famines and earthquakes' (Matt. 24:7). God calls such a time a 'day of darkness… thick darkness' (Joel 2:2), a dark gloomy day. And there is nothing to be seen in all the confusions around us in the world today except for the frogs and the unclean spirits that are going forth to stir up the lusts of men in order to make havoc of one another (Rev. 16:13, 14).

(4) It adds greatly to the difficulty of a season when we have no sense of where it is things are heading or of what will be their consequences. We have usually two ways by which we may have some idea of how things will transpire: by observing God's providence and the likely consequences it indicates, and by the rule of Scripture. The truth is that we are presently in a time when no one is able to discern what future is indicated by our circumstances. What will be the result of all these things? Whether it will be the deliverance of the church, the desolation of the nation with the further troubling of the church, or whether God will bring good out of our circumstances in this generation or at some other time, no-one knows. This makes it a dark season. 'We do not see our signs' (Psa. 74:9)—we have no indications of what God intends to do, 'and there is none among us who knows how long.'

Any one of these factors would make the way difficult and the season one of darkness, but when they all concur together that would greatly increase the difficulty. I think that they are all upon us presently.

Secondly, what are the evident signs of the approach and departure of such a season?

There are three signs or outward evidences of an approaching difficult season.

(1) One evident sign is when God's patience is abused. Thus, as in Ecclesiastes 8:11: 'Because the sentence against an evil deed is not executed speedily, the heart of the children of man is fully set to do evil.' It happens in this way: men fall into wickedness, great wickedness; their consciences

accuse them and they are afraid; the strength of their lusts carry them into the same sin again and their consciences begin to grow a little colder than before; no evil comes of it and judgment does not fall speedily; and so their hearts at last become wholly set on doing evil. Onlookers say, 'These men are given up to evil. Surely judgment will speedily come upon them.' But when the judgment does not materialise, when God is patient, they themselves turn as wicked as the former. The abuse of God's patience is a clear providential sign of a season of God's displeasure. And if ever it was visited upon any, it is visited upon us; and men realize it more and more every day. Everyone talks of other men's sins, and seeing no judgment fall upon them they give themselves up to the same sins.

(2) Another sign is when God's warnings are despised. 'O LORD, your hand is lifted up, but they do not see it' (Isa. 26:11). This is a difficult season indeed, for Isaiah continues, 'Let the fire for your adversaries consume them.' Never have any people received as many warnings as we have: warnings in heaven above and on earth beneath; warnings by lesser judgments and by greater, and warnings from the word. God's hand has been lifted up, but who takes notice of it? Some despise it and others talk of it as a tale to be told, and that ends the matter. Who is there who sanctifies God's name in all the warnings that are given to us? 'The voice of the LORD cries to the city' (Mic. 6:9), but only the man of 'sound wisdom' sees God's name in these cries of his to the city, in his warnings from heaven and earth, signs and tokens, great proclamations of his displeasure.

(3) A third sign is the tendency of all kinds of people to feel secure and take no notice of these things. I have spoken of this subject of security before and I pray that God would warn us all with respect to it. I believe that we are all not such strangers to our own hearts as to know that for all these warnings we are yet inclined to this false security. If God did not prevent it we should fall fast asleep notwithstanding all the judgments that are around us.

Any one of these things would reveal that we are under a difficult dispensation of providence, but when they all concur—God be merciful to such a people! It is an opening of the door so as to release judgments to the uttermost.

Now if we do truly live in such a time (as, I think, we are all convinced of), then, thirdly, what shall we do? What are the special duties with respect to our entering in to, and passing through, such a season?

I might speak of the particular exercise of those graces that are needed at such a time: such as faith, resignation to the will of God, readiness for his pleasure, waiting upon God, being weaned from the world, and such like, but I will instead give you three or four duties, which are particularly relevant for such a season.

(1) Our first duty is that we should meet together and talk about these things, Mal. 3:16, 17. This is a good plan for a dark time, as some of us have previously experienced. The day of the Lord, burning as an oven, was coming:

> Then those who feared the LORD spoke with one another. The LORD paid attention, and heard them, and a book of remembrance was written before him of those who

feared the LORD and esteemed his name. 'They shall be mine,' says the LORD of hosts, 'in the day when I make up my treasured possession, and I will spare them as a man spares his son who serves him.'

When was this? At a time of great judgment and great sin: when they called 'the arrogant blessed. Evildoers not only prosper[ed] but they put God to the test and they escape[d]' (Mal. 3:15).

It is our great duty, as we have opportunity, to speak with one another about these things; about their origins and causes—how much of them arise from the unbelieving, wicked world; how much from the persecuting, idolatrous world; and (which concerns us most of all) how much from the professing church. By so doing we must see how we can sanctify God's name in it. We might have as much advantage as any others under heaven for fulfilling this duty if we only made use of that 'money' that God has put into our hands (Prov. 17:16), but if we are 'fools,' and have no 'sense' to improve it, the fault will be ours.

You have the opportunities for meeting and assembling, but I fear that your private meetings have much coldness of affection. I wish this were not so. It may be that some thrive and grow. I hope so. If God would help us to order the church aright as we ought to do, there might be no better time than now, under our present circumstances. We are in great need of voluntary self-examination, and may the Lord not lay it to our charge that we have neglected this for so long. Much lack of love might have been prevented, many duties fulfilled and many evils removed, if we had come up to the light that

God has given to us. But we are at a loss, and God knows we suffer for it, because of not discharging our duty.

The first thing, then, is to speak often one to another; to sanctify the name of God by a humble, diligent inquiry into the causes of this dispensation, and to prepare ourselves for these things.

(2) The second duty at such a time is for every one of us privately to resort to Jesus Christ in prayer and supplication: 'What shall be the end of these things?' You have a notable example of this in Daniel 8:13, 14:

> Then I heard a holy one speaking, and another holy one said to the one who spoke, 'For how long is the vision concerning the regular burnt offering, the transgression that makes desolate, and the giving over of the sanctuary and host to be trampled underfoot?' And he said to me, 'For 2,300 evenings and mornings. Then the sanctuary shall be restored to its rightful state.'

I imagine that there is something of the ministry of the angels here—one holy one speaking to another holy one, and an answer being given to Daniel. But the first holy one who spoke was Jesus Christ—the derivation of the word is 'One that reveals secrets'. An application was made to Jesus Christ, the revealer of secrets, to know how long. And often in Scriptures, at difficult times, you will find the request of the saints to God: 'How long?,' 'How long shall it be till the end of these wonders?,' 'O my LORD, what shall be the outcome of these things?' (Dan. 12: 6, 8). A humble application by faith and prayer is made to Jesus Christ to know the mind of God with respect to these matters so as to satisfy our souls. Do not leave yourselves to wander in your own thoughts and imaginations. It is impossible for us not to be arguing things and trying to give a rational account of them, but this will never bring satisfaction. But if we go to Jesus Christ and ask him: 'O Lord, how long?' he will in secret grant satisfaction to our souls.

This then is the second thing—speak together about these things, and press Jesus Christ to give satisfaction to your souls concerning these dark times.

(3) Another specific duty required in an evil day is to mourn for the sins that are in the world. This is recommended to us in Ezekiel 9. When God had given a commission to the sword to kill both young and old, he spared only those who groaned 'over all the abominations' of the city. We fail in this duty; we are not affected by the sins of the worst of men around us; by God being dishonoured; by the Spirit of God being blasphemed; by the name of God being reproached through them. We ought to groan over all these abominations. We mourn for the sins of God's people, but we ought also to mourn for those abominations that others are guilty of, for their idolatries, murders, bloodshed, uncleanness—all the abominations that fill our own country and also those countries around us. It is our duty at such a season to mourn for them, otherwise we do not sanctify God's name, and we shall not be found prepared for the hard providences of God which are coming to us.

(4) The fourth and last specific duty is that we hide ourselves. How do we do that? The storm is coming. Get

an ark, just as Noah did when the flood was threatening his world. His example is given as a precedent for all future judgments. Two things are required in order to find an ark—fear and faith.

(a) Fear: 'By faith Noah... in reverent fear constructed an ark' (Heb. 11:7). If he had not been moved with fear of God's judgments he would never have provided an ark. It is a real complaint against us that we are not moved enough by the fear of God's judgments. We talk of the most fearful things that can befall human nature, and expect them every day, yet we are not moved with fear. 'Yet neither the king, nor any of his servants... was afraid,' said Jeremiah, 'nor did they tear their garments' (Jer. 36:24). Habakkuk, when he foresaw God's judgments, reacted very differently (Hab. 3:16): 'I hear, and my body trembles; my lips quiver at the sound; rottenness enters into my bones: my legs tremble beneath me. Yet I will quietly wait for the day of trouble.' This is the way to find rest in the day of God's judgments. We are afraid of being thought of as cowards because of fearing his coming.

(b) And we cannot properly provide an ark for ourselves unless we are guided by faith, as well as being moved by fear. 'By faith Noah... constructed an ark.' You have heard of all the reasons for encouraging our faith: the name and properties of God, the accomplishment of the promises of God. Because of all these attributes, encourage your faith to construct an ark. But you will say: 'We still do not understand what you mean by constructing an ark and hiding ourselves. "The prudent sees danger and hides himself"' (Prov. 22:3). God calls us to enter our chambers and hide ourselves until the fury has passed by. If we knew what this was we would take ourselves there.

I will give you one example of what I mean. Do not let your minds have any rest until, by some renewed act of faith, you have a strong and clear impression of the promises of God upon your heart, and of your interest in those promises. If it were only one promise, it would prove an ark for you. If, under all these dark dispensations, moved by fear and acting by faith we can obtain a renewed sense and pledge of our interest in even one of the promises of God, that will prove an ark over us which will endure, whatever the storm to come. Think of this, and apply your minds to it, so that you do not wander up and down in uncertainty. Make every effort to obtain a renewed pledge of your interest in some special promise of God—that it belongs to you—and it will be an ark in every time of trouble that befalls you.

12. Preparation for Christ's coming in times of judgment

In our last meeting we discussed what is required in us in a time of approaching judgment and calamity. God was pleased to guide us to the discovery of the necessary exercises of many graces, and the necessary fulfilling of many duties for such a time. We intend today to spend our time praying that God would give us those graces and stir them into exercise in us by his Spirit. We will ask that he would help us so to perform those duties that when the Lord Christ shall come, in any holy dispensation of his providence, we should be found in peace in him. This is to be the main emphasis of our prayers today, together with our usual prayers for ourselves, the church and the nation.

Let me mention some things that might encourage us to pray:

The Scriptures everywhere, on all occasions, call us particularly to specific preparation, by the exercise of grace, for reformation and holiness. 'For it is time for judgment to begin at the house of God' and 'what will be the outcome for those who do not obey the gospel of God' (1 Pet. 4:17). What, then, is our duty? Why, he says, 'since all these things are thus to be dissolved [all the outward frame of this world], what sort of people ought you to be in lives of holiness and godliness?' (2 Pet. 3:11). Brothers, we ought at all times to attend to lives of holiness and godliness, but, says the apostle, the approach of judgment provides an extra motivation—'since all these things are thus to be dissolved.' It is true that since Christ has died for us, washed us in his blood and given his Holy Spirit to us, 'what sort of people ought we to be?' But this greatest of motives does not exclude extraordinary occasions but reinforces them. 'Watch yourselves lest your hearts be weighed down with dissipation and drunkenness' (Luke 21:34), with any excessive use of our creaturely comforts. What if this might be the case? Then, 'that day [will] come upon you suddenly like a trap'—the day when all shall be dissolved—the day of approaching calamities. We ought at all times to consider these things, but if our minds are not influenced particularly by the thought of the approach of that day, we are not his disciples.

I would also mention those places where God express-es his great displeasure against those who do not make particular efforts of preparation when calamities are approaching. Isaiah 22:12-14: 'I called for mourning, fasting and wearing sackcloth, and you took yourselves to feasting on all occasions.' 'Surely,' said the Lord, 'this iniquity will not be atoned for you until you die' (verse 14). It was reckoned as among the sins of the most immoral persons that when God's hand was lifted up and ready to strike, they would not see it, and so failed to learn righteousness (Isa. 26:10, 11).

Let us therefore beg for grace. Though God multiplies warnings, makes appearances of mercy and then writes death upon them, and entangles everything in darkness, yet our work of preparation proceeds so slowly. Cry earnestly to God for those supplies of grace and Spirit that may effectually bring us to him; that we might no longer remain in our present state.

Three things are required of us with respect to approaching judgment, and we cannot pass through or properly fulfil one of them, to our own comfort and to God's glory, without specific and extraordinary preparation.

Firstly, that we ourselves stand in the breach, to turn away the threatened judgments. Secondly, that we may be ready for deliverance, if it pleases the Lord in his grace to give it to us. As Christ said, speaking of great calamities, 'raise your heads, because your redemption is drawing nigh' (Luke 21:28). And thirdly, that if they fall upon us we may go through the calamities cheerfully and comfortably.

These three comprehend all the requirements for the various threats of approaching judgments that encompass us presently. There is not one of them that we can be fit for unless our hearts and lives undergo an extraordinary preparation. I do not know whether these things are believed or not, but they will soon be found to be true.

Thus, for the first requirement, who is the man who would dare to propose himself to stand in the breach to divert judgment from the nation? Anyone who dares do this would have to be prepared by these things we have discussed, having good and comforting assurance of his own personal interest in Christ, having freed himself from those sins that have brought down the judgments, and living a life resigned to the will of God. We would be provoking God if we thought we could do this work when we ourselves are involved in bringing down the judgment upon us.

Secondly, we cannot be ready for deliverance unless we are appropriately prepared. I have heard views preached, which, the more I consider the more I dislike, that teach that God, in delivering his people, works for his own name's sake and so that he might have all the glory, and that it shall be seen to be all of grace. Therefore he will sometimes deliver his people even when they are in an unreformed and unreforming state, so that he might shame them and afterwards humble them by his mercy and grace. But I do not know of any Scriptural principle upon which this view may be based nor one instance of an example which would confirm it.

But here is the truth: God will deliver his church, not-withstanding all their sins and unworthiness, even without any previous humbling of themselves, only when two things concur. Firstly, when God has fixed and limited a certain season in his word, and has provided a promise for their deliverance. And secondly, when before that deliverance they lack the means of humbling themselves. God delivered the children of Israel out of Egypt when they were in a very bad condition—an ignorant, stubborn, faithless generation—but both these things concurred: God was engaged by his promise that at the end of four hundred and thirty years he would visit and deliver them; and they were deprived of all ordinances of worship in Egypt. Not a sacrifice could they offer while they were there; not a Sabbath (I believe, though it is not mentioned in Scripture) could they observe; the way of worship and of knowledge of God was taken from them. So also when God delivered the children of Israel out of Babylon they were not in a good condition, but here also God was committed by promise that at the end of seventy years they should be delivered; and in Babylon also they had no means of instruction or reformation—no temple, no sacrifice—these were denied. But there are no examples of God delivering any people out of their distress when they had refused to be reformed and humbled, or to turn to him even though he had supplied all the means of grace necessary for humiliation, reformation and turning. It is vain for us therefore to expect anything of this nature. If indeed we had been thrown for many years into a wilderness situation, and had no preaching, no assemblies, no administration of ordinances, no warnings or charges from God, we might have expected that the Lord would have given us deliverance; yet having had all these things but not making the use of them, we have no ground to expect this. Therefore I confess that I know of no rule, instance or example to give me hope of deliverance until God comes in to work a thorough change and reformation in our hearts and lives. Thus it is so necessary that we prepare to meet God in a way of judgment.

The third thing that may lie before us is for us to go cheerfully through the calamities that may overtake us. This is what we considered in our previous discussion. Even the best of us, who have long been followers of Christ, will be very sadly surprised when the days of calamity come if we have been negligent in complying with the calls and warnings of God that we have received to bring us into better frames. We shall find our strength will fail us, our comforts will flee from us, and we shall be left to inward darkness when outer darkness increases, and not know how to lose our sorrows.

These things, brothers, I thought it my duty to tell you, so that, if it be the will of God, they may be of use to you to throw away all those false hopes and expectations with which we are so ready to feed ourselves in such a day as this. It is high time for us to be calling on God.

13. The contest between Christ and Antichrist

The prophet Daniel tells us that when he understood by books (namely, the writings of the prophet Jeremiah) the time that had been appointed for the great contest between Babylon and the church, 'Then,' he said (Dan. 9:3-15), 'I turned my face to the LORD God, seeking him by prayer and pleas for mercy with fasting and sackcloth and ashes.' And if you read his prayer you will find nothing of confidence, nothing of self-praise, but only a deep acknowledgment of sin. 'We, our kings, our princes, our fathers, [and our church,] have all sinned,' so that 'to us belongs open shame.' And the church had never before experienced such shame as that which would have come upon them if they had been disappointed at this time. But, he adds, 'to you belong mercy and forgiveness.' He acknowledges that everything depended on 'mercy and forgiveness,' even though he knew by the books that the time had come.

Truly, brothers, we do not know by any Scripture or revelation, as he did, that the time has come in which the long contest and conflict between Babylon and the church will be decided. But it looks as if this is so as we view the book of providence, and so much like it, that it is a plain duty that we should give ourselves to prayer and supplication. If we do not, we may experience that open shame that belongs to us because of our sins. It is that contest which we are now considering and which seems to be coming to a head. It is the greatest battle that ever was, with the one exception of that contest between the person and gospel of Christ on the one hand and the devil and the pagan world on the other. Next to that is this contest between Christ—in his offices and grace, in his gospel and worship—and Antichrist. And today that battle is engaged to as great an extent as ever. The question to us and to our posterity is: Will it be Christ, or Antichrist? The worship of God, or the worship of idols? Whether the outpouring of the Spirit of God in his worship, or every kind of superstitious imposition? This is the present contest and it may be that there was never a more striking example, under heaven, of the engagements of this war than will be the case in these nations in these days. (I am not saying that it will happen soon or in the immediate future, but you all know that this is the true state of affairs.)

I mention all this so that you may know that more than just an ordinary spirit of earnestness and fervency of spirit and wrestling with God for Zion's cause, the kingdom of Christ and the defeating of his enemies, is required from us presently. What God will work we do not know. If he should be at work, he has said (Rev. 12) that when a flood was cast out of the mouth of the dragon to swallow up the woman (and we have had such a flood from the dragon's mouth against the whole interest of Christ in this nation), the earth lifted herself up and helped the woman and turned aside the flood. Good old Eli's heart trembled for the ark of God. The interest of God and the truths of Christ are still among us but besieged by the Philistines. Whether they will be taken by them, I do not know—God only knows. But truly, brothers, our hearts ought now to tremble for the ark of God, that God would keep it among us, and not give his glory into the hands of the adversary.

I have mentioned these things for one purpose: that if God wills it, in this great conflict between Christ and Antichrist, our hearts may be a little warmed on all occasions to contribute our prayers to the help of the Lord and of the ark of the Lord; that we may see a blessed result to this trial and not be covered with that shame and confusion of face that belong to us.[1]

14. Christian duty under divine warnings

Before proceeding with our discussion, I would ask you a few questions:

[1] The following quotation, taken from *The Nature and Causes of Apostasy from the Gospel* published by Owen in 1676, shows his understanding of the national movements of his time and the context in which this reference to Antichrist is to be understood. Historically, the twenty-year period immediately prior to the writing of these questions had witnessed the restoration of the Stuart monarchy (1660), the oppressive 'Clarendon Codes' (1661–65), the 'Act of Uniformity' and the 'Great Ejection' (1662). Owen equated Antichrist with the Roman Catholic Church (see p. 70-4) but his words are relevant to all ecclesiastical and national movements that draw men away from true Biblical worship to that which is man-made.

'It is not unknown how ready many, yea multitudes, are in all places to desert the whole protestant faith and religion, casting themselves into the baffled, prostituted remainders of the old apostasy. Every slight occasion, every temptation of pleasure, profit, favour, preferment, turns men unto the Papacy; and some run the same course merely to comply with the vanity of their minds in curiosity, novelty, and conformity unto what is in fashion among men. Some flee unto it as a sanctuary from guilt, as that which tendereth more ready ways for the pacification of conscience than that faith and repentance which the gospel doth require. Some having lost the sense of all religion in the pursuit of their lusts, finding themselves uneasy in their atheism, or disadvantaged by the reputation of it, take shelter in the Roman dress. Some are really entangled and overcome by the power and subtlety of numerous seducers who lie in wait to deceive. By one way and means or another, on motives known to themselves and him who useth them as his engines to subvert the faith, many in all places fall off daily to the Papacy, and the old superstition seems to be upon a new advance, ready to receive another edition into the world; yea, it is to be feared that there is in many places such a general inclination unto a defection, or such an indifference to all religion, that multitudes want nothing but a captain to conduct them back into Egypt… By such means are the numbers of apostates multiplied amongst us every day.' (*Works*, Vol. 7, p. 73)

Firstly, do you think that there are extraordinary calls and warnings of God towards our nation at this time? Secondly, if you do indeed think so, what is the message being conveyed by these calls?

Thirdly, do you think that any group of people, believers or churches are exempt from paying attention to and obeying these calls of God? For there is a reserve, a reticence to acknowledge these calls, lying upon our hearts. The nation is very wicked (I shall not repeat its sins) and the warning is very general. God testifies his displeasure against the nation, the body of the people. Now my question is whether there is any rule whereby we, who profess ourselves believers, and a church, should count ourselves exempt from any particular compliance with these extraordinary warnings? Do we believe they are for others and not for us? And yet: 'when disaster brings sudden death, he mocks at the calamity of the innocent' (Job 9:23). It was the good figs that went first into captivity (Jer. 24:1-7).

Fourthly, what have we done so far by way of a proper response and answer to these calls of God, which we have acknowledged before him? We have been speaking of them and I think I can say that we have good and sincere desires to respond appropriately. I would not reflect badly, beyond what the evidence suggests, on any individual or of the church. We have had good intentions and sincere endeavours, but it may well be that they have not been in any way suitable or proportional to the present occasion. And I must conclude therefore that, in any eminent and extraordinary way, we have done nothing. We have not yet inquired what we should do and what in particular the Lord our God requires of us, nor have we declared our design and purpose for a universal compliance with these great calls of God for repentance and for turning to him.

I mourn over myself night and day; I mourn over you continually. I do not see that life and vigour in returning to God that I would wish for, not in ourselves nor in our associated churches. And allow me to say, from the experience of my own heart, I am jealous over you.

We might later proceed to consider some appropriate outward duties but we have not yet come that far, we have only considered in our hearts what we have done to respond to God's calls, to reform and change our hearts and change the vigour of our spirit in walking with him. I would speak as tenderly as I can so that no one might take offence, and I would acknowledge to you that I myself have not attained. Nor can I, though I am making every effort to bring my heart to that frame which God requires of us at all times. I find so many obstructions. If you have attained, I shall rejoice with all my heart and soul, but if not, help those who are labouring after it. All I intend now is to settle on our souls a strong conviction that we have not as yet answered the calls of God in the heart.

I hope that eventually we may go on to consider all the ways and instances by which we might reform and return to God, but in the meantime, I offer you this: that unless we lay a foundation for it by a deep and broken sense of our past miscarriages and present conditions, and unless we see in the church some evidence of a renewed spirit of vigour and earnestness, then I shall be very despondent over this matter. But rather, let us be persuaded that we will lay down such a foundation: an acknowledgement that it is our duty, as the first thing that God aims at by his many calls, to arrive at a deep sense upon our hearts of our past miscarriages and of our present dead, wretched frame. Ought we not to lay that foundation here? Well then, let us apply ourselves to it. It may be that though some do have a deep and humble sense of their past failings, yet that is not the case with all of us, and what we seek is the edification of the whole. Therefore, brethren, it is our present duty to labour to affect our hearts deeply with this necessary conviction.

Let us, therefore, pray every day that God would keep this subject in the thoughts of our hearts, not only in our own hearts but in those of us all. When you think that you have reached an end of your thoughts on this, consider that phrase of the Holy Spirit, as expressed by David: 'O LORD God of… our fathers, keep this forever in the imagination of the thoughts of the heart of thy people' (1 Chron. 29:18), that is, 'in the first internal framing of our thoughts'. There must be a continuing framing and *coining* of thoughts (if I can put it like that) in us to this purpose. And I recommend this to you, that if this is a truth, and we are convinced that it is our duty to labour to affect our hearts with a sense of the guilt of our souls, and to adjust the frame of our minds, to the will of God and the holiness of Christ, who is coming to visit his churches, then, 'What sort of people ought you to be?' Not such as we have been. We have to work hard to obtain a sense of this and I hope you will not object to it. For, believe me, if any of us have any corruption, temptation or disinclination in our spirits that conflicts against this, then all our endeavours will be in vain, unless we first lay this foundation.

I know that one great means for beginning and helping along this work is by earnest crying to God—days of prayers and supplications and humiliations. I am loath to find the remedy here. I have seen so many days of humiliation without any resulting reformation that I dare not see this as our remedy. We shall surely make use of such days, as God will help us. I wish the church would indeed keep such days, if they find in themselves a sense of duty and a heart crying to God in sincerity and truth. I have now been a long time in the ministry of the word (though very unprofitably) and I have seen churches established, and I hope that I shall never see them ending in a confidence which is merely a profession, and in the formal observation of duties of humiliation. God knows, I have often thought of this, and I have no confidence that our salvation lies there. Let us have as many days of humiliation as we have hearts for, and no more; as many as shall truly result in reformation, but no more. But let us all begin with ourselves; and who knows, God may give wisdom to this, our church. I am ready to faint, and to retire, and I beg of the church that they think of some other person to lead them instead of me, someone without my disadvantages. The last day will reveal that I have nothing in my heart except to lead you in the ways of God—to the enjoyment of God.

PART II:
DIFFICULT AND DANGEROUS TIMES

*But understand this: that in the last days there will come
times of difficulty*—2 Tim. 3:1

Y OU know that my usual practice upon these occasions
is to speak as plainly and familiarly as I can with respect
to our present circumstances, and this is what I plan to do,
God helping me in my weaknesses.[1]

The words of the text contain a warning of imminent
dangers. There are four things involved:

(1) The nature of the warning: 'But understand this.'
(2) The evil of which they are warned: 'Times of difficulty.'
(3) How this evil will be introduced: 'There will come.'
(4) The time and season of it: 'In the last days.'

(1) The nature of the warning

'*But understand this.*' Paul is saying: 'To all the other
instructions that I have given you, Timothy, as to how

[1] This sermon was preached on a day (September 3, 1676) that was set
apart for solemn fasting and prayer.

you should conduct yourself in the house of God so that you may serve as an example to all future ministers of the gospel, I must add this: "But understand this." It is part of your duty and office to be aware of and to consider the impending judgments that are coming upon the churches' (cf. 2 Tim. 3:1-8).

Therefore, so as to justify the purpose of this sermon, I will lay down the following premise: that it is the duty of all ministers of the gospel to take notice of any dangers into which the churches are falling. May the Lord help us, and all other ministers, to be awake to this part of our duty! You know how God emphasises in the parable of the watchman (Ezek. 33) that we are to warn men of approaching danger. He has given us this certain law: If we warn the churches of their approaching dangers we discharge our duty; if we do not, their blood will be required at our hands. God's Spirit foresaw our tendency to be negligent in this area and so the Scripture lays it down as a duty to be performed, on the one hand, and as a requirement of the people's blood at the hands of the watchman if the duty is not performed, on the other. We find it performed by the prophet Isaiah, 'He cried, a lion: my LORD, I stand continually upon the watchtower' (Isa. 21:8). A lion is an emblem of approaching danger. So also the prophet Amos, 'The lion has roared; who will not fear?' (Amos 3:8). It is the duty of gospel ministers to warn of impending dangers.

The apostle in speaking to Timothy is speaking to all of us; 'You also must understand this.' It should be the great concern of all believers and all churches to have their minds focused on all present and approaching dangers. We have inquired so much about signs, tokens and evidences of relief and deliverance, and all kinds of other things, that we have almost lost the benefit of all our trials, afflictions and persecutions. It is the duty of all believers to be aware of present and imminent dangers. 'O LORD,' said the disciples, 'what will be the sign of your coming?' (Matt. 24:3). They were focused on his coming. Our Saviour answered, 'I will tell you: (a) There will be an increase of errors and false teachers. Many will say, 'Look, here is Christ,' and 'Look, there is Christ.' (b) There will be a falling away from holiness: 'Lawlessness will be increased, the love of many will grow cold.' (c) There will be great distress among the nations: 'Nation will rise against nation, and kingdom against kingdom.' (d) There will be great persecutions: 'Then they will deliver you up to tribulation and put you to death, and you will be hated by all nations for my name's sake.' (e) There will be great tokens of God's wrath from heaven: 'Signs in the heavens, the sun, moon and stars.' The Lord Christ wished to inform believers of how they should look for his coming; he told them of all the dangers. Concentrate on these things. I know that you tend to overlook them, but these are the things that you are to focus on.

To be unaware of a present time of difficulty is to be guilty of that complacent sense of security which the Scriptures condemn so often. I will emphasise three points for you, briefly:

(a) It is that attitude of heart which God detests and abhors above all others. Nothing is more hateful to God than a secure, complacent heart in difficult days.

(b) I do not fear to say, and will do so to the day of judgment, that a complacent person in difficult days is certainly under the power of some predominant lust, whether that seems to be the case or not.

(c) This secure, senseless attitude is a certain omen of approaching ruin. Understand this, brethren, I pray that you will understand this, for the sake of your souls and mine, that you will be aware of, and affected by, the perils of the season before us. What these are, if God helps me and gives me strength, I will show you by and by.

(2) The evil of which they are warned

'*Times of difficulty*.' Paul is warning of a particular evil and danger, namely, hard times, perilous times, difficult times, like those of public plague when death lies at every door; times that I am sure we will not escape, whenever they might fall. I shall say no more now in that this will be my main point later.

(3) How this evil will be introduced

'*There will come*.' We have no word in English that expresses the force of ἐνστήσονται (*henstēsontai*). In Latin, it is '*immineo, incido*'—the descent of a bird upon its prey. God's hand is in this business. These times shall so come—they will be so decisive in their coming—that nothing can keep them out. They shall press themselves upon us and prevail. It would be wise for us, therefore, to recognize God's displeasure in difficult times, in that God's judicial hand is to be seen in them, and we recognize in ourselves reason enough why they should come. But when is it that they will come?

(4) The time and season of it

'*In the last days.*' These words 'latter' or 'last days' are used in three ways in Scripture: sometimes for the times of the gospel, as opposed to the time of the Jewish theocracy ('In these last days he has spoken to us by his Son,' Heb. 1:2); sometimes for the days of the consummation of all things and the end of the world; and often for the latter days of the church ('The Spirit expressly says that in later times some will depart from the faith,' 1 Tim. 4:1; 'Little children, it is the last time: and as ye have heard that antichrist shall come, even now there are many antichrists; whereby we know that it is the last time,' 1 John 2: 18). It is this third meaning that is intended here in 2 Timothy 3:1. Yet, you may take it as having any of these meanings, i.e. the last days—the days of the gospel; the last days—towards the consummation of all things and the end of the world; or even, the last days after the formation of the Reformed Church, our own churches; or even again, the last days of our own individual lives. In whatever sense the words are taken, it is time for us to look out for that which is to come in the last days.

However, the main observation from this text upon which I shall concentrate is:

> When churches have continued faithful in their profession for a time and then begin to fall into decay, dangerous times shall overtake them, which will be hard for them to escape—'But understand this, that in the last days there will come times of difficulty.'—2 Tim. 3:1

My purpose is to get you to think a little of the nature of such days and to show the variety of factors that can produce a difficult season. I want you also to consider our duty with respect to such a season, both as regards particular difficulties and difficult times in general. What we must not say is that which was once said of the prophet Ezekiel, 'He prophesies of times far off' (Ezek. 12:27). I do not prophesy of things a great way off; no, I shall speak of things that are even now upon us; things that we see and know, that are as clear as if written by the beams of the sun.

(1) The first thing that marks out a period as being difficult is when men profess to maintain true religion outwardly but are clearly under the predominance of horrible lusts and wickedness. And the reason why I put this first is because the apostle himself does so, in our text. 'There will come times of difficulty.' Why?

> For people will be lovers of self, lovers of money, proud, arrogant, abusive, disobedient to their parents, ungrateful, unholy, heartless, unappeasable, slanderous, without self-control, brutal, not loving good, treacherous, reckless, swollen with conceit, lovers of pleasure rather than lovers of God, having the appearance of godliness.—2 Tim. 3:2-5

They maintain their profession of the truth of religion under an evident predominance of visible, vile sins, and an ongoing practice of those sins. This resulted in a time of difficulty. You decide whether or not we presently are in a similar time (And, in passing, let me add that we should and ought to witness against it, and mourn for the public sins of the days in which we live. It is as glorious a thing to be a martyr for bearing testimony against the public sins of a particular period, as it is for bearing testimony to any of the truths of the gospel.)

Under these circumstances, the times are difficult and dangerous, for the following reasons:

(a) Because there is so much danger of infection. Believers and churches may become infected by it. The historian, Thucydides, wrote of the plague at Athens in the second and third years of the Peloponnesian war, from which multitudes died.[2] Of those who lived, few escaped without losing a limb or part of a limb—some an eye, others an arm or a finger—the infection was so widespread and terrible. And truly, brothers, where this plague comes, a plague of the evident practice of unclean lusts under an outward profession of faith, though men do not die of it, yet one will lose an arm, another an eye or a leg, because of it. The infection spreads even to the best of believers, more or less. This makes it a dangerous and difficult time.

(b) They are dangerous because of their effects, for when predominant sins have broken all the bounds of divine guidance and rule, how long do you think human rulers can keep matters under control? In a time such as the apostle describes, men's sins will break out on all sides, and if they break through human restraints as they have broken through God's restraints, they will bring about ruin and confusion everywhere.

[2] *Thuc.* Book II.47-8.

(c) They are dangerous because of their consequences, namely, the judgments of God. When men do not receive the truth in love but have pleasure in unrighteousness, God will send them a strong delusion to believe what is false. This is how 2 Thessalonians 2:10, 11 describes the way in which the Papacy came into the world. Men professed the truth of religion but did not love it—they loved unrighteousness and ungodliness—and God sent them Popery. That is the meaning of these verses, according to the best commentators. Do you profess the truth, but at the same time love unrighteousness? The result will be a sense of security, when under superstition and ungodliness. This is the end of such a dangerous time. The same argument applies when God sends temporal judgments as a consequence.

What is our duty at such a time?

(a) The first is that we ought to mourn for the public abominations of the world and of our own country. In Ezekiel 9:4 we read that God sent out his judgments and destroyed the city. But before doing so, he put a mark on the foreheads of the men who sighed and groaned over all the abominations committed in the city. You will find this passage referred to in the Book of Revelation: 'Do not harm the earth or the sea or the trees, until we have sealed the servants of our God on their foreheads' (Rev. 7:3). It is those who 'groan over all the abominations committed' in the land who alone are God's servants, whatever other men may profess. The 'groaners' of Ezekiel 9 are 'the servants of God' of Revelation 7. And truly, brothers, we are much to blame in this matter. We have almost been content that men should be as wicked as possible, and we sit still to see what will become of it. Christ has been dishonoured, the Spirit of God blasphemed, and God provoked against our country, and yet we have not been affected by these things. I can sincerely say, thank God, that I have at times been distressed at heart by this. But I am afraid that we all come short of what is our duty in this regard. 'My eyes shed streams of tears, because people do not keep your law,' said the psalmist (Psa. 119:136). Our eyes have seen, and our ears heard, horrible profanities against God's name and horrible abominations of behaviour, and yet our hearts have been unaffected by them! Do you think that this is how God wishes us to react at such a time? Not to be affected by it all, and not to sigh over the public sins of the land? God's servants will groan. I might mention, but am not free to do so, the various prejudices that keep us from mourning over public abominations, but they will be easily suggested to your thoughts, particularly those that have kept us from concentrating on this duty of mourning for public sins. Let me say that, according to the Scripture rule, none of us have any foundation for believing that we shall escape the outward judgments that God will send because of these sins, if we have not been mourners and groaners over them. Rather, the outward dispensation that will fall upon us, may be as sharp a revenge as that which will encounter those most guilty of them. Nothing in the Scripture teaches to the contrary. How God will deal with us, I do not know.

This, then, is one part of our duty today—that we should humble our souls for all the abominations that are committed in our country and for our lack of mourning over them.

(b) Our second duty is that we should take care that we are not infected by the evils and sins of a difficult time. One might think that the opposite would be the case but, in reality, what I have observed is that (unless there is an extraordinary dispensation of God's Spirit) as some men's sins grow very high, other men's graces grow very low. Our Saviour has told us, 'Because lawlessness will be increased, the love of many will grow cold' (Matt. 24:12). You might think that an increase of lawlessness in the world would move Christians to love one another much. 'No,' says our Saviour, 'the opposite will be found to be true: as some men's sins grow high, other men's graces will grow low.'

There are reasons for this:

(i) At such a time we tend to have light thoughts of great sins. Jeremiah considered it a dreadful thing that when Jehoiakim threw his roll of prophecy into the fire to be burned, 'Yet neither the king nor any of his servants who heard all these words was afraid, nor did they tear their garments' (Jer. 36:24). They had become hardened to both sin and judgment. When men, however wise they might be, become hardened to sin, they will soon become hardened to judgment. And I am afraid that the great reason why so many of us have no impression upon our spirits of the danger and perils of the days in which we live is because we are not aware of sin.

(ii) People tend to excuse their own lesser evils when they see every day the greater wickedness of other men. There are some, even, who pay tribute to the devil—they live their lives in the midst of such awful sins and so excuse their own lesser sins. This is part of the public infection: that they 'do not join them in the same flood of debauchery' (1 Pet. 4:4), yet live in omission of duty, in conformity to the world and in many foolish, damaging and foul lusts. They justify themselves with this: that others are guilty of such greater sins.

(iii) Let these people remember that to socialize generally with the world, at such a time as this, is full of danger and peril. Most professors take on the same colour and complexion as those in whose company they spend their time.

This is the first thing that makes a particular period dangerous. I do not know if such things are of concern to you; they seem so to me, and I must tell you of them.

(2) A second dangerous time, and one which is difficult to avoid, occurs when men are prone to leave the truth, and seducers are all around, ready to gather them up. These two things will always go together. Do you see the multitudes of these enticers? You can be certain that there is always a tendency for the minds of men to forsake the truth, and where this abounds you will never lack tempters—those who will help to lead men's minds away from truth. This is because both God and Satan are at work. When God sees men grow tired of the truth and willing to leave it, he, in judgment, leaves them. And Satan strikes at such occasions, stirring up seducers. This makes a time dangerous. As the apostle describes it, 'Now the Spirit expressly says that in later times [these difficult days] some will depart from the faith by devoting themselves to deceitful spirits and teachings of

demons' (1 Tim. 4:1). This is Peter's warning also, 'there will be false teachers among you, who will secretly bring in destructive heresies, even denying the Master who bought them, bringing upon themselves swift destruction. And many will follow their sensuality' (2 Pet. 2:1, 2). Times full of danger will come which will draw men away from the truth and into destruction.

If you should ask how we are to know, at any particular period, whether there is a tendency in men to depart from the truth, let me mention three ways by which we might judge the matter:

(a) The first is given in the letter to Timothy: 'The time is coming when people will not endure sound teaching, but having itching ears they will accumulate for themselves teachers to suit their own passions' (2 Tim. 4:3) When people grow tired of sound teaching—when it is too plain, too heavy, too dull, too common, too high, too mysterious, or one thing or another that does not please them, and they want to hear something new, something pleasant—that is a sign that here is an age in which there are many who are ready to leave the truth. And we know many like this.

(b) A second indication is found when men have lost the power of truth in their lives and conduct, and are just as ready to part with the profession of it in their minds. Can you see a man maintaining the profession of the truth when living in a worldly way? All he needs is the bait of a temptation, or the work of a seducer, and his faith will be taken away from him. An inclination to listen to novelties, and the loss of the power of truth in one's life, are signs of this tendency to decline from the truth. Such a time is dangerous, because the souls of many are destroyed by it. This was the apostle's warning: 'there will be false teachers among you, who will secretly bring in destructive heresies, even denying the Master who bought them, bringing upon themselves swift destruction' (2 Pet. 2:1). Will it remain there? No. 'And many will follow their sensuality, and because of them the way of truth will be blasphemed' (2 Pet. 2:1, 2). Brothers, while all is well with us, through the grace of God, and our own houses are not in flames, do not let us think that the times are not dangerous when so many are turning to Popery and Quakerism, into sensual errors, and falling into swift destruction. Would you say that a time of public plague was not dangerous just because you were still alive? No. Would you say that a fire was not dreadful, just because your own house was not burned down? No; you would believe it to be a dreadful plague, a dreadful fire. Well then, should we not think that this is a dangerous time when so many are tempted to depart from the truth, and when God in his judgment has allowed Satan to stir up so many tempters to draw them into their destructive ways, so that their poor souls might perish forever?

Such a time is also very prone to produce indifference in those who would not forsake the truth utterly. I never thought that I should ever have lived in this world to find the minds of believers brought to complete indifference as to the doctrine of God's eternal election, the sovereign efficacy of grace in the conversion of sinners, and justification by the imputation of the righteousness of Christ. Yet, many have become indifferent with regard to all these things; they do not know whether they are true or not. I bless God that I knew something of a previous generation, when believers would not hear of such indifference without detesting it greatly, but by now influential believers are the leaders in such indifference, and it is too much present even in the best of us. We are not as concerned for the truth as were our predecessors. I wish I could say that we are as holy as they were.

(c) Such a tendency to depart from the truth is an indication of a dangerous and difficult season because it is the greatest evidence of the withdrawing of God's Spirit from his church. The Holy Spirit was promised for this purpose, 'to guide us into all the truth' (John 16:13), and when the effectiveness of the truth begins to weaken, that is the clearest indication of the departing and withdrawing of the Spirit. This is surely dangerous, for if the Spirit of God departs then our glory and our life depart.

What then is our present duty at such a time? Warnings of danger are given in order to instruct us in our duty.

(a) The first is that we should not be content with what we judge to be a sincere profession of the truth, but make every effort to be found exercising all those graces that particularly relate to the truth. If these are not found in our hearts, our profession will be ineffective. These are:

(i) To love the truth. 'Because they refused to love the truth' (2 Thess. 2:10). They professed the gospel, but they did not receive it as something to be loved. There was a lack of love for the truth. Truth will do no good to any man, if he does not love it. 'Speaking the truth in love' (Eph. 4:15), is the heart of our Christian profession. Brothers, let us make every effort to love the truth, and to remove all prejudices in our minds so that we might do this.

(ii) To labour to have the experience of the power of every truth in our hearts. Isn't this the way you have learned Christ? How? By 'put[ting] off your old self, which belongs to your former manner of life and is corrupt through deceitful desires... put[ting] on the new self, created after the likeness of God in true righteousness and holiness' (Eph. 4:20-23).

(iii) To be full of zeal for the truth. Truth is the most proper object for zeal. We ought to 'contend for the faith that was once for all delivered to the saints' (Jude 3); to be willing, as God helps us, to part with our name and reputation, to undergo scorn and contempt—all that this world can throw at us—while giving testimony to the truth. Everything that this world counts dear and valuable is to be forsaken, rather than the truth. This was the great purpose for which Christ came into the world.

(b) Keep firmly to the means that God has appointed and ordained for your preservation in the truth. I see some that are ready to fall asleep, having no concern for these things. May God wake up their hearts! Keep to the means for being kept in the truth—namely, the present ministry of the word. Bless God for the remaining ministry that values the truth, knows the truth, and is sound in the faith; cleave to it. There seems to be very little influence upon men's minds from this ordinance and institution of God—this great work of ministry. Yet, realize that there is much more to it than that the ministers seem merely to have better abilities for arguing and speaking than your-self, that they possess more knowledge, more light, better understanding than you. If this is all that you believe is in the ministry you will never benefit from it. But these men are appointed by God; the name of God is on them; God will be sanctified in them. They are God's ordinance for preserving the truth.

(c) Let us remember the faith of those who went before us in this nation, in the testimony of previous generations. I sometimes think that there never was a more glorious testimony to be found on earth over a thousand years than was among the Christians of the last age in this country. And what was the nature of their faith? Were they half Arminian and half Socinian; half Papist and half I don't know what? Remember how zealous they were for the truth; how little would their holy souls have accepted of these public defections from the doctrines of the truth that we see in our day, yet think nothing of them nor mourn over them. God was with them, and they lived to his glory and died in peace; 'whose faith follow' (Heb. 13:7), and whose example pursue. And remember the faith that they lived in and died in. Look round about you and see if any of the new creeds have produced a new holiness that exceeds theirs.

(3) A third dangerous and difficult time occurs when believers mix with this world and learn its manners. And if those first two dangerous seasons have come upon us, this one has also. This was the foundation and source of the very first difficult time experienced by the world—that which first brought in a flood of sin and then a flood of misery.

It was the beginning of the first great apostasy of the church and resulted in the severest mark of God's displeasure. 'The sons of God saw that the daughters of man were attractive. And they took as their wives any they chose' (Gen. 6:2). This is just one instance of the church of God, the sons of God, believers, mixing with the world. It was not only that they took to themselves wives, but they represented one instance related by the Holy Spirit of the church degenerating and mixing with the world. What is the result of such mixing? 'They mixed with the nations' (Psa. 106:35). And what then? 'And learned to do as they did.' If anything under heaven will produce a dangerous time this will—when we mingle with the world and do as they do.

I will mention two things on this point: the ways in which believers mix with the world; the danger of it.

(a) Believers mingle with the world in those things which properly belong to the world. They do not mix readily with what is clearly of the devil, but rather with those things in which the world is seen in its own colours.

For example, *a corrupt speech*, which is the spirit of the world, the result and fruit of a vanity of the mind by which the world is corrupted and corrupts. The devil has his hand in all this but it is the world and the spirit of the world that produces corrupt speech. And how this spreads among believers! Light, vain, foolish speech! A man's whole life may be spent in it; not just on one occasion or another, but almost always and upon all occasions, everywhere!

The *vain habits and dress of the world* are other instances. The habits and attire of the world are those things by which the world shows itself for what it is. Men may read the evident characteristics of the world by what it wears and how it behaves. They are blind who cannot read vanity, folly, uncleanness and luxury in the way the world dresses. The declension of believers in imitating the ways of the world in these matters produces a dangerous time: it is a mingling where we learn to do as they do; and the judgments of God will be the result.

And thirdly, we grow like the world when, on all occasions, we are *as regardless of the sins of the world as they are*, and as little troubled by them. Lot lived in Sodom but 'torment his righteous soul over their lawless deeds that he saw and heard' (2 Pet. 2:8). Wherever we might live, is it the case that our souls are so tormented, that we cannot receive all the ways of the world—all its great abominations—with the same receptive spirit as the world?

We have not mentioned the *sensual living* and other things that characterize this sad mixing with the world which believers are engaged in at this present time: corrupt speech, ostentatious dress, unawareness of the sin and abominations of the world around us; these are to be seen in believers as much as in the world. We have mixed with the nations and learned to do as they do.

(b) And such a time is dangerous because the sins of believers in it are directly contrary to the whole design of Christ's mediation in this world. Christ gave himself for us that he might redeem us from all lawlessness and to purify for himself a people for his own possession (Tit. 2:14). 'You are... a royal priesthood, a holy nation' (1 Pet. 2:9).

Christ brought down the hatred of the devil and of all the world upon himself and against himself, in order to take a people out of this world and make them a holy people for himself. For them then to throw themselves again into the world is the greatest contempt that they can show to Jesus Christ. He gave his life and shed his blood to recover us from the world, and we throw ourselves back in again. How easy it would be to show that doing this opens an avenue to all other sins and abominations and, as I truly think, to show that because of this God's indignation and displeasure will soon reveal itself against the believers and churches of our day! If we will not be different from the world in its ways, we shall not long be treated differently from them with regard to privileges. If we are the same as the world in our walk, we shall soon be so in our worship, or, perhaps, have no worship at all.

As to our duty in such a difficult and dangerous time, let me leave you with three warnings, and may the Lord fix them upon your hearts:

(a) To profess religion and to perform duties while our conversation is just like that of the world is nothing but a degraded way of leading men blindfold into hell. We must not talk of little things when engaged in such a cause.

(b) If you wish to be like the world, you must expect the world's fate. Your future will be the same as the world's future. Read and discover, throughout the pages of the Bible, what lies ahead for the world—what God's thoughts are towards the world. Does he not say, 'If it lies in wickedness it shall come to judgment; the curse of God is upon it?' If, therefore, you wish to be like the world, you must accept for yourself the world's destiny. God will not separate.

(c) Lastly, consider that by such behaviour we will have lost the most glorious cause of truth that there ever was in the world. I do not know of a more glorious cause, since the days of the apostles, than that committed by God to his church and people in our nation, in its purity of doctrine and ordinances, but we have lost all its beauty by this mixing with the world. I truly think that it is high time that the congregations in this city, by their elders and representatives, should consult together how to put a stop to this evil, which has brought about the loss of all the glory of our testimony. It is a dangerous time when believers mix with the world.

There are other dangerous times which I had intended to discuss but I will just mention them:

(4) When there is a great attendance on outward duties, but inwardly there is just spiritual decay. Now, my brothers (which most of you in this congregation are, I hope, by the grace of God—in sincerity, though in much weakness), you know how often I have preached on the causes and reasons for inward decays, and the means to be used for recovery. Therefore, I shall not spend time on this again.

(5) Times of persecution are also times of danger. It is not for me to tell you whether such times are upon us or not; it is your duty to decide. Whether or not there is an outward retaining of the truth under an evident prevalence of abominable lusts in the world; whether or not there is a proneness to forsake the truth, and seducers at work to draw

men away from it; whether or not we are mixing with the world, and thereby learning to do as they do; whether or not there are inward backslidings under an outward fulfilling of duties; whether or not many are suffering under persecution and trouble; all these you must judge, and act accordingly.

A few more words of application and I will end.

Application 1

Let us all receive the exhortation to impress upon our hearts the dangers of the day in which we live. You have heard a poor, weak sermon on this topic and perhaps it will be quickly forgotten. O that God would be pleased to give us this grace: that we might realize that it is our duty to have our hearts affected by the dangers of our times! A time of storm at sea is no time to be asleep on top of the mast! In order that this might be the case:

(1) When you consider the events of the day, bring them before the rule of God's word, and see what God says of them. We hear this and that story of some great and horrible wickedness, we discuss it in conversation at the next opportunity, and then we forget it. We hear of the judgments of God abroad in the world, we consider them in the light of our own standards, and then we pass them by. We do the same with the distresses of others, discussing them and then forgetting them.

But brothers, when you see all these things happening in the world around you, if you want to have your hearts impressed by them, bring them to the word. See what God says of it. Speak to God about it. Ask and inquire at the mouth of God what he has to say of these evils and judgments—this coldness of heart among believers, their mixing with the world and learning its ways. You will never have your hearts affected by the situation until you come and speak to God about it. And then you will find it represented as in a mirror in a way that will make your hearts ache and tremble.

(2) If you wish to be aware of the present dangers, do not focus upon yourself. While your greatest concern is yourself, or the world, all the angels in heaven will not be able to make you aware of the danger of the days in which you live. If you are chasing after riches or honour, if you concentrate upon yourself, nothing can make you sensible of the perils of the day. Therefore do not focus upon yourself.

(3) Pray that God would give us grace to be aware of these dangers. Believe me, this is a great grace. Plead this in your private prayers and in your family prayers. May God help us in our public prayers to petition him that he would make our hearts aware of the dangers into which we have fallen!

Application 2

There are two aspects to a difficult time—the sin of it and the misery of it. Make every effort to be aware of the first, or you will never be aware of the second. Though judgments lie at the door; though the heavens be dark over us and the earth shake under us, as it does today; though no wise man can see where he might build for himself a safe dwelling; yet, we can talk of these things and hear of other nations soaking in blood; we may receive tokens of God's displeasure—warnings from heaven above and the earth beneath—and still no one seems to be aware of them. Why is this? Because we are not sensible of sin, nor ever will be, unless God makes us so.

I shall list the sins that we should be aware of under three headings: the sins of the poor, wretched, perishing world; the sins of believers in general; our own particular sins and declensions. Let us strive to have our hearts affected by these. There is no purpose in telling you this and in telling you that judgment is approaching; no purpose for your leaders and those on the watchtower to cry, 'A lion, my lord; we see a lion.' Unless God makes us aware of sin we shall not be aware of judgments.

Application 3

Remember that there is a special frame of mind required of us at such dangerous times. What is that? A spirit of mourning. O that frame, that *cheerful* frame of spirit that is upon us! May the Lord forgive it, the Lord pardon it, and keep us in a humble, broken, mournful spirit. This is that particular grace that God looks for at such times. When he will pour out his Spirit there will be great mourning, together and apart. But now, we have to confess, there is no mourning. God help us, we have hard hearts and dry eyes, even when considering all these dangers before us.

Application 4

Keep up the watchfulness of the church with all diligence and by rule. And when I say *rule* I mean a *living* rule. There is nothing that I fear more than that God should withdraw himself from his own institutions because of the sins of the people, and leave us with only the carcass of outward rule and order. Why does God give rule and order? For their own sakes? No, but so that they might be the clothing for faith and love, meekness of spirit and a heart of compassion, watchfulness and diligence. If these have gone, then all outward rule and order may go, however excellent they are. Maintain a spirit that will continue to be alive and easily affected. Get a spirit of watchfulness over the church—not a watchfulness that is ready to jump at faults, but that is ready to watch over the souls of men diligently, out of pure love and compassion, to be ready to do all the good we can to them.

As it was with a poor man who took up a dead body and tried to get it to stand, and it fell; and set it up again, and it fell again, so that he cried out, 'It needs something within,' to quicken it and give it life—so it is with church order and rule. You may set them up as often as you wish but they will all fall if there is not love for one another and pleasure in one another's progress. 'Exhort one another every day, as long as it is called "today", that none of you may be hardened by the deceitfulness of sin' (Heb. 3:13).

Application 5

Understand that in such times as these, not all of us will escape. There is never any mention of a difficult season in Scripture without it resulting in some losing their faith, others following their sensuality and still others turning aside. Brothers and sisters, for all you know it may be you or me who falls! Let us double our watch, each one of us, for the time has come upon us in which some of us may fall, and in falling will experience much pain. I do not say that we shall perish eternally—God deliver us from going into the pit!—but some of us may fall so as to lose a limb or some other member, and our works will be committed to the fire that shall burn them all. God has kindled a fire in Zion that will test all our works, and we shall see in a very little time what will become of us.

Application 6

Lastly, remember that great rule which the apostle provides for such times as these, 'But God's firm foundation stands.' O, blessed be God for it! 'The LORD knows those who are his' (2 Tim. 2:19).

What, then, is required on our part? 'Let everyone who names the name of the LORD depart from iniquity' (2 Tim. 2:19). Your profession, your privileges, your light, will not keep you safe; you are gone, unless every one that names the name of Christ departs from all iniquity. What multitudes of those who profess a faith perish every day! O that our hearts could bleed in seeing poor souls in danger of perishing, though they might profess the sincerest faith.

Let me sum up all that we have heard. Difficult times and seasons are coming upon us; many are wounded already; many have failed. The Lord help us! The crown is fallen from our head. The glory of our testimony is gone. The time is short. The Judge stands before the door. Take this one word of advice, brothers, 'Stay awake at all times, praying that you may have strength to escape all these things that are going to take place, and to stand before the Son of Man' (Luke 21:36).

PART III:
LIVING BY FAITH IN DIFFICULT TIMES

T HIS work is made up of four sermons on living by
   faith, describing:

- (1) the use and advantage of faith in a time of national
  adversity;
- (2) the use and advantage of faith in a time of reproaches
  and persecutions;
- (3) the use and advantage of faith in a time when Roman
  Catholicism is on the increase;
- (4) the use and advantage of faith in a time when true
  religion is declining.

Sermon 1: The use and advantage of faith in a time of national adversity

The righteous shall live by his faith—Hab. 2:4

This is the first time that these words are mentioned in
the Scriptures but they are later quoted three times by the

apostle Paul. It is as if Paul preached three times on the verse—in Romans 1:17, in Galatians 3:11, and in Hebrews 10:38.[1] The verse is full of heavenly truth and is made use of by the apostle for different purposes. I do not know of any other text that has been more preached on, or more written about, by those who have discussed the life of faith, than this one: how the righteous live the life of justification, how they live the life of sanctification, the life of consolation, the life of peace, of joy, of obedience, etc. My purpose is quite different, and it agrees with the purpose of the prophet in this first use of the words, as we shall see.

You know that for many years, without fail, I have been warning you continually of an approaching time of distress and have discussed the sins which have occasioned this. When this time will come, the LORD knows—I do not know the year or the month. But I have told you that 'it is time for judgment to begin at the household of God' (1 Pet. 4:7); that in the last days of the church 'times of difficulty' will come (2 Tim. 3:1); that God seems to have 'made us wander from his ways and hardened our hearts, so that we fear him not' (Isa. 63:17); and that no-one knows what the power of his wrath will be. In all these things I have warned you of troubled, distressing, difficult times, and all men now realize that these lie at the door and will shortly enter in upon us. But now I must change my approach, and my present work, both now and, God willing, on future occasions, is to show

[1] In volume 1 of his seven-volume commentary on the letter to the Hebrews, Owen provides a 31-page defence of the Pauline authorship of the Letter. John Owen, *Hebrews* (repr. Edinburgh: Banner of Truth Trust, 1991), pp. 65-95.

how we should conduct ourselves in the distressing circumstances that are coming upon us and which may, perhaps, almost overwhelm us.

What this text teaches us is that, when an overwhelming distress approaches, *we ought particularly to live by our faith.* That is the meaning of this verse.

That this is our duty is seen from this passage and its context. In the previous chapter the prophet had received a vision—a dreadful vision—from God of the approach of the Chaldeans and of the destruction they would visit upon the church and all the land. Having received this vision he considers, in the light of it, what his own duty should be and what the duty of the church should be. 'As for me,' he says, 'I will take my stand at my watchpost and station myself on the tower, and look out to see what he will say to me, and what I will answer "when I am reproved"' (Hab. 2:1). 'God will reprove me; there will be great argument between God and my soul. I know my own guilt and sin, and I need to be prepared to have something to answer God when I am reproved—something that I may cling to. The remedy,' he says, 'to which I shall cling is this, "the righteous shall live by his faith."'

Two things are involved here:

Firstly, he says, 'I will cling *to Jesus Christ for righteousness'* (this is how Paul uses the passage). 'I have nothing else with which to answer God when I am reproved.'

Secondly, 'I will pass through all these dreadful and terrible dispensations that are coming my way by living the life of faith,'—*a particular way of life*, as we shall see. When the flood was coming upon the world, Noah was 'a herald of righteousness' (2 Pet. 2:5). What righteousness did Noah preach? Well, just that righteousness which he had himself, for he 'became an heir of the righteousness that comes by faith' (Heb. 11:7). When the flood was coming, Noah preached the righteousness of faith to the world, so that they might escape if they only listened to it. But they rejected it. Therefore, at the approach of a distressing or calamitous time, there is, in a particular and special way, a living by faith required of us.

Now, you will say: 'What is a calamitous season?' or 'What do you mean by a distressing time?' I will mention two things which describe the kind of times that I judge to be evidently calamitous:

(1) When it *exceeds the bounds of what we think of as affliction*, or when the dispensations of God's anger in it are more than we can conceive of as being merely afflictions. For example, in Ezekiel 21: 9, 10, 13:

> Son of man, prophesy and say, Thus says the LORD, say: A sword, a sword is sharpened and also polished, sharpened for slaughter, polished to flash like lightning! (Or shall we rejoice? You have despised my rod, my son, with everything of wood)… For it will not be a testing—what could it do if you despise the rod?

The *rod* represents all affliction, but God will bring a *sword*—a judgment that cannot be reduced to the category of affliction. Therefore, whatever cannot be reduced to an affliction—a distress falling upon a nation or the church of God—but a visitation in which there is a general experiencing of *anger, judgment and wrath*—that is a calamitous time.

(2) When judgments fall indiscriminately upon all sorts of people without distinction, that also is a calamitous time, because it strips men of all the comforts they cherish in their own minds. 'It is all one; therefore I say, He destroys both the blameless and the wicked' (Job 9:22). What? Is this what God always does? Does he never make a distinction in his judgments? Yes, sometimes; but 'when disaster brings sudden death, he mocks at the calamity of the innocent' (Job 9:23). When God brings a scourge or sword that will slay indiscriminately, that will seize upon, destroy and devour the innocent so that they shall not escape, he will be as someone who stands by mocking, watching how they conduct themselves under trial.

This is enough of a description to show what I mean by a distressing, calamitous time—it cannot be reduced to the category of affliction, and it slays indiscriminately amongst the good and the wicked. It may even be that it is the good figs that shall go first into captivity (Jer. 24: 1-7). I cannot see any reason why that might not happen, and, in that new situation, God might have purposes of mercy for them.

In this sermon I shall discuss, firstly, how we should live by our faith—how we should conduct ourselves; what faith will do at such a time; and what our duty is as these distressing times approach. Secondly, how faith acts and conducts itself under other perplexities and distresses that are either upon us or that we fear shall come.

Faith guides and acts in the soul, at the approach of distressing times, in the following ways:

(1) It will give a soul a *reverential fear of God* in his judgments. This was the experience of the saints of old, Heb. 11:7, 'By faith, Noah, being warned of God... in reverent fear (εὐλαβηθεὶς, *eulabētheis*) constructed an ark.' Every man, unless he is very hard of heart and far from righteousness, on being warned by God, will become full of a reverential fear of God in his judgments. This was the case with David, 'My flesh trembles for fear of you, and I am afraid of your judgments' (Psa. 119:120). He was not afraid of the external judgments, but when experiencing them he trembles with a reverential fear of God. It was the same with the prophet Habakkuk when given the vision of the approach of the Chaldean army; 'I hear, and my body trembles, my lips quiver at the sound; rottenness enters into my bones; my legs tremble beneath me. Yet I will quietly wait for the day of trouble to come upon people who invade us' (Hab. 3:16). He had a reverential fear of God in his judgments working within him.

According to my observations of our present state, most people may be divided into one of three groups:

(a) There are some who are *truly afraid* of approaching judgments. They do not know how soon these will reach them or their families, their relations and possessions—everything for which they have worked and have exerted their utmost care and industry. The flood that will arrive at their door, ready to carry everything before it—they fear it every day. Some men also die for fear of dying; they are poor for fear of poverty—they will part with nothing because they are frightened of having to part with everything. This is a strange self-contradiction! It is not the way that faith works. To the extent that this fear works in our spirits, God will reprove us for it, 'Who are you that you are afraid of man that dies, of the son of man who is made like grass, and have forgotten the LORD, your Maker... and you fear continually all the day because of the wrath of the oppressor' (Isa. 51:12, 13). And you have not regarded the Lord of hosts as holy and not made him your fear (Isa. 8:13). Who are you? God hates this sinful fear; it is an abomination to him. This is nothing but the fear for self; we wish to keep everything warm around us while we are in the world, and we are afraid of anything that might destroy.

(b) There are others who *utterly despise* these things, who take no notice of them whatsoever. They do not think that any kind of distress will ever come upon them—and if it does, they think that they shall cope well enough with it. They have 'made a covenant with death, and with Sheol they have made an agreement.' They say that 'when the overwhelming whip passes through it will not come to us' (Isa. 28:15). They have a thousand ways of distracting themselves from all the distresses and troubles that are approaching. This attitude swallows up most of mankind and is what the prophet reflects upon: 'Your hand is lifted up, but they do not see it. Let them see your zeal for your people, and be ashamed' (Isa. 26:11).

(c) A third group is mentioned in Judges 5:6 and may be called *byways men*, idle talkative men, that have nothing better to do than to walk up and down and talk. They are not concerned with the reverence of God and with his judgments. They talk as if there were no God in heaven who sees them, or as if they had nothing to do with him. If we have the least true saving faith at work in us it will throw out this cursed attitude from our hearts; it will be daily banishing it from our souls and bringing us to that which is its proper work, as I have mentioned. 'The LORD,' says the psalmist, 'has made himself known; he has executed judgment' (Psa. 9:16). But the things which God does make known of himself in his judgments which he executes on the world are very little considered. These attributes, which he specifically reveals in these dreadful dispensations, are his majesty, his holiness and his power.

God will appear as awfully *majestic* and wonderfully *glorious* at such troubled times. He speaks of himself on such an occasion, 'In that day mankind will cast away their idols of silver and their idols of gold... to the moles and to the bats, to enter the caverns of the rocks and the clefts of the cliffs, from before the terror of the LORD, and from the splendour of his majesty, when he rises to terrify the earth' (Isa. 2:20, 21). If we have the light of faith to illuminate it, we shall see a majesty and a glory in God's acts, even those of his public and troubling judgments—such a greatness and glory that the soul will be constrained to bow down before him.

God, in his judgments, also manifests his *holiness*, which we shall comment on later. Thus, in Revelation 15:4, 'Who will not fear, O LORD, and glorify your name? For you alone are holy.' And how is this known? 'For your righteous acts have been revealed.' When God reveals his judgments, his holiness will appear. So, when Habakkuk pleaded with

God with respect to the great invasion of the Chaldeans (the context of my text) he cried out, 'O Lord my God, my Holy One... You who are of purer eyes than to see evil' (Hab. 1:12, 13).

In his judgments God also glorifies *his power*. He establishes one, pulls down another, and does whatever he pleases. In this way he reveals clearly his sovereign power.

Now, to live by our faith is to throw away all those cursed attitudes mentioned previously and to maintain this attitude in your heart as the foundation for everything that will follow, namely, a reverential fear of the majesty, holiness and power of God. Without this we shall not please God in anything that we do. If there is any other attitude within us, these times of trouble will pierce us to the very soul before they are over.

(2) Then, secondly, where faith has filled the soul with a reverential fear of God, its first work will be to bring the soul *to prepare and provide an ark for itself.* This is what happened in the great example mentioned: 'Noah... in reverent fear constructed an ark for the saving of his household' (Heb. 11:7). Whatever men may pretend, unless they are blinded by a careless stupidity and complacence (which, I fear, is true for so many professors of faith), they cannot avoid preparing some means of hiding from such troubles. 'What shall we do when this comes upon us?' They have some means of escape in mind. A rich man will look to his wealth—this is 'his strong city' (Prov. 18:11). He may lose a great deal, but he will save enough for himself. A strong man trusts in his strength; a wise man in his wisdom. In

one way or another, men will prepare something to be an ark for them when the storm comes. Those who do not do so will dash to and fro in utter uncertainty, but hoping still that in some way, but exactly how they do not know, they will be delivered from all their troubles; that what this minister or that prophet tells them will not take place and that, somehow or other, they shall escape. But this is not how you prepare an ark—only a work of faith can prepare successfully. So let us consider two things: 1. What is this ark that has to be prepared? 2. How are we to enter into it, with respect to an approaching calamity?

(a) *This ark is Jesus Christ.* Faith in him is necessary. In this second chapter of Habakkuk, when the prophet on his watchpost asks God what to do as the overwhelming flood of the Chaldeans approaches, he is told, 'The righteous shall live by his faith.' What is that? It is to look for righteousness by Christ; to seek afresh for justification and life by Christ. There is no other way, no other ark. And he is described as this ark in that well-known passage: 'A man (that is, Jesus Christ) shall be as an hiding place from the wind, and a covert from the tempest; as rivers of water in a dry place, as the shadow of a great rock in a weary land' (Isa. 32:2). That is the ark. I do not know any better way to describe what I mean by securing ourselves in the ark than this description given by the prophet, though expressed in such metaphorical language. We have a similar picture of Christ in Micah 5:5. Having given the promise of Christ, Micah adds, 'And [this man] shall be their peace when the Assyrian comes into our land.' To take ourselves to this ark is to approach the fountain of our peace. We find the picture also in Psa. 2:12: What to do when 'his wrath is quickly kindled'? And the answer: 'Blessed are all who take refuge in him;' who trust in him. In whom? In the Son—'Kiss the Son.' Surely, brothers, the wrath of God is now quickly kindled, and greatly so, in many different ways. The indications of God's wrath are felt by men of all kinds: believers, those in the world, in their own individual lives, in all societies, in all relationships. Where then are we to take ourselves other than to Jesus Christ? 'Blessed are all who take refuge in him.'

(b) But it would not have been of any advantage for Noah or his sons if there had been an ark prepared for them which did not have a door. 'Make a door,' said God to them, 'so that you may have an entrance.' (cf. Gen. 6:16) To obtain an interest in Jesus Christ is the main work of our faith throughout all the days of our lives. But how are we now to obtain a *specific entrance* into this ark, Jesus Christ, appropriate for the situation and conditions in which we find ourselves at this season when troubles and calamity are fast approaching? I know of only one way to accomplish this and that is by means of *a solemn renewing of our covenant with God*. This is the way that has been used by the church from the foundation of the world, without exception—that in order to be delivered from any storm that was gathering, they entered into the ark by renewing their covenant with God. And in that the hour has come, we must therefore enter *once again* into this ark, Jesus Christ. In civil matters there is no wisdom in rejecting an expedient unless we have something better with which to replace it, and it is exactly the same in spiritual matters. I would ask all who fear God to stir up their hearts and thoughts and offer to us, if they can, any better method for our church, or any church, of entering into safety at this time, and we would embrace it. But as a church we have chosen this way, though I begin to fear that some of you look upon it as a very dead, sluggish approach, one that you do not really know how to handle. But do not be mistaken; in the sight of God there is no better way that you could have taken. Do not be despondent; the day is approaching when others 'shall take hold of the robe' of your skirts, 'saying, "Let us go with you, for we have heard that God is with you"' (Zech. 8:23).

Some—blessed be God, and let his holy name be exalted!—have gone much further ahead of us already, in zeal, warmth and courage, under a sense of the approaching trials. I do not look for any safety or deliverance in the trials and afflictions ahead, except for what is obtained by believing. I see no help in anyone who thinks otherwise. Bless God, who has provided for us this door of entrance before the flood comes and the rain falls. Bless God for it, I say, and make use of it, and be able to plead it before him. And let God know that you have made him your choice; that you are under his protection and not that of the world. I do not say that you will be saved *in time*, but you shall be saved *to eternity*. I cannot say that you will have peace *with men*, but you shall have peace *with God*. I cannot say that you will not lose your *lives*, but I will say that you shall not lose your *souls*—and they are our greatest concerns. Make sure of your entrance. A door set in the ark will do you no good unless you enter through it and are sure of your entrance. And how are we to make sure of our entrance so that we shall be safe? Because unless we do this, we are not exercising faith. Well, by fulfilling our duties—committing ourselves to the performance of those duties that God requires of us. There are no new things required of us but only those special duties of the new covenant, which have already obtained you entrance into the ark, within which God will give you all the rest that may be received in this world. This is another of the acts of faith necessary at the approach of times of trouble.

(3) If we live by faith at a time of approaching trouble this will stir us up to *search and examine our hearts* as to whether we have given any welcome to those sins which have brought down these judgments upon us. This is what faith—if it is in any way sincere—will always produce in us. And this is what God now particularly requires of us. The sins which do provoke such judgments are of two kinds: the public and shameful sins of the world; the sins of churches and believers.

(a) Public and *shameful sins of the world.*

The apostle lists them (1 Cor. 6:9, 10): 'Do not be deceived: neither the sexually immoral, nor idolaters, nor adulterers, nor men who practice homosexuality, nor thieves, nor the greedy, nor drunkards, nor revilers, nor swindlers will inherit the kingdom of God.' He does so again in Ephesians 5:5,6, 'For you may be sure of this, that everyone who is sexually immoral or impure, or who is covetous (that is, an idolater), has no inheritance in the kingdom of Christ and God... for because of these things the wrath of God comes upon the sons of disobedience.' He lists them also in Galatians 5:21, 'Now the works of the flesh are evident: sexual immorality, impurity, sensuality, idolatry, sorcery, enmity, strife, jealousy, fits of anger, rivalries, dissensions, divisions, envy, drunkenness, orgies, and things like these.' There is a wonderfully clear exhibition of these texts in our country today: every man may read an exposition of such sins in the behaviour of people around us. Some will say that they bless God they are free of such things, and in this way they hope that they themselves have had no part in bringing down the judgments of God that are upon us. Let these fall, they say, upon those who are guilty of such provocative abominations; those against whose ungodliness the wrath of God is revealed from heaven. It is good if they are not guilty of any of these sins, but the seed and foundation, even of sins like these, lie *in our nature* even if they are not found *in our persons*, and we do not know what the rebelliousness of our nature may have contributed towards provoking the eyes of God's glory. And even though you may have escaped these pollutions that are in the world through lust, there are other sins.

(b) *Sins of churches and of believers*

These have just as much effect in bringing down judgments, with respect to Christ's *mediatory* kingdom, as the worst sins of the world have for procuring judgments in his providential kingdom. I know of a time when, in a storm, a complete ship and all who were in it were in danger of being lost, and the cause of the storm was just the one man, Jonah, who was in the ship at the time.

I shall just list these judgment-provoking sins of churches and believers under the titles given to them in Scripture:

(i) *Lukewarmness;* which was the judgment-procuring sin of Laodicea; being content with outward order and freedom from scandal; the sin of Sardis and one which will prove ruinous to the best churches in the world. (ii) *Lack of love* among ourselves, and division in churches. (iii) *Earthly-mindedness*, love of the world, and conformity to the world, which is found among the majority of believers.

Sermon 2
The use and advantage of faith in a time of reproaches and persecutions

The righteous shall live by his faith—Hab. 2:4

You may remember that I have previously preached to you from that verse of the psalmist, 'Clouds and thick darkness are all round him; righteousness and justice are the foundations of his throne' (Psa. 97:2). At that time we considered what should be our particular duties when clouds and darkness surround us, as they do today. And some of you, I know, have been persuaded that the clouds gathering will fall, at least in their first approach, upon the people of God. I must repeat this again and again. I have been warning you for some years and telling you that this will happen. The present attitude of my own soul (against which I have to fight); that attitude which I have observed in others; the state and condition of all churches and believers, so far as I can see, is this: we have become dreadfully complacent. I speak from the heart and from what I know of our present state and of the state of God's cause. We have fallen into a dismal sense of security. This confirms my belief that the storm will come upon us and that it will not be long before we feel it. My purpose therefore is to show you how we should behave under the perplexities and difficulties which we shall have to fight against in this world. I have not had to study to find examples to present to you, but will share with you the experiences of my own heart.

I have already described our duty as these distressing times approach. I will now, secondly, show you how faith acts under other various difficulties that are now present or are coming upon us, namely:

• How we are to live by faith under all the reproaches and persecutions that may befall us on account of the order and fellowship of the gospel and of the form of God's worship which we profess (this sermon).

• How we are to live by faith with reference to the returning of antichristian darkness and cruelty, should God allow it to be so (sermon 3).

• How we are to live by faith under an apprehension of the great and sad decline in churches, in church membership, and in believers, and in the gradual withdrawal of God's glory from among us because of these (sermon 4).

How are we to live by faith *with respect to all those reproaches*, that scorn and contempt, which is poured out against the ways of God which we profess, against that worship of God in which we engage, and against that order of the gospel which we observe, together with the persecution that will follow on this account? I can truly say, as the Jews said of Christianity to Paul, 'With regard to this sect we know that everywhere it is spoken against' (Acts 28:22). The whole world seems to be in agreement that the name of Israel should, in this way, be forgotten. Very few people are concerned about these matters, while presently all is well with them, with their families, estates and inheritances. If the ways of God are censured, what is that to them? They are not involved in this. They do not say, as the psalmist does when speaking in the person of Christ, 'The reproaches of those who reproach you have fallen on me' (Psa. 69:9). Perhaps some of us are more aware than others (or at least, we should be) of the recriminations that are continually cast against Christianity, in that we are included in this recrimination. But to those not concerned by this scorn and contempt I would say three things:

Firstly, *what evidence do you have that you have any interest in God's glory?* These things which are criticized and censured are exactly those things by which God is glorified in this world. And if you are not concerned for them, as they suffer so much opposition, what evidence is there that you have any part at all in the glory of God?

Secondly, *what evidence do you have that you have any love for these things*, if you can hear them reproached, criticized, condemned, and never be moved by it? An honest, good man on hearing his wife or children being reproached with lies and shameful accusations would be concerned because of his love for them, but for those who can hear the ways of God reproached every day and not be concerned about it, so long as all is well with them and theirs, such people can have no evidence that they love God's ways. On one such occasion, Nehemiah cried out, 'Hear, O our God, for we are despised. Turn back their taunt on their own heads and give them up to be plundered in a land where they are captives' (Neh. 4:4). God has made special promises to those who feel the reproach in this way. 'I will gather them,' he says

(Zeph. 3:18). Who will he gather? 'Them that are sorrowful for the solemn assembly… to whom the reproach of it was a burden' (Zeph. 3:18). The solemn assemblies were being scorned and mocked and there were some of them—not all—to whom this reproach was a burden. 'These,' said God, 'I will gather.'

Thirdly, I will add one more word. If you are not concerned for the reproaches that are thrown at the ways of God, *persecution will wake you up*, and either make you concerned or put an end to your profession of belief.

What we must look into is how, under these difficulties with which we fight, are we to glorify God and pass through them without loss and to our spiritual advantage?

The apostle, describing this very situation in the tenth chapter of Hebrews, directs us as to what to do. 'You endured a hard struggle with sufferings,' he says, 'sometimes being publicly exposed to reproach and affliction, and sometimes being partners with those so treated. For you had compassion for those in prison, and you joyfully accepted the plundering of your property, etc' (Heb. 10:32-34). But how shall we act under such conditions? 'Well,' he says, 'my righteous one shall live by faith' (verse 38).

What is the work of faith in this condition, so that we may glorify God and persevere to a good and comforting position? It is to call your own hearts to account, and to understand how faith can support you. I will tell you what I am endeavouring to do in my own heart, and may God guide you to find any way more useful! What will faith do in such a case? Let me answer:

(1) *Faith will give us such an experience of the power, efficacy, sweetness and benefit of the gospel ordinances and gospel worship that will cause us to despise all that the world can do against us.* This is where I will cast my anchor, and would encourage you not to be confident in yourselves—for nothing else will keep and preserve you. A well-grounded opinion and judgment will not keep you; love to this or that man's ministry will not preserve you; your own ability to argue for your beliefs will not save you. I can give you instances where all these have failed. Resolutions that if all men should leave God's ways, you would not, will only let you down. Nothing can preserve you but a sense and experience of the usefulness and sweetness of the work of the gospel, according to the mind of Jesus Christ. It is only faith that can give you this. 'Long,' says the apostle, 'for the pure spiritual milk' (1 Pet. 2:2). That is, 'Desire and labour to continue in the ordinances of the gospel and the worship of God according to the directions of his word.' And how may you do that? Only 'if you have tasted that the LORD is good' (verse 3), otherwise you will never desire it. I must hope that through the grace of God (for there is no other way) I might yet continue (if still kept alive) in a constant experience of exercising faith in God, delighting in him, loving him, under the effects of his word, while I come to that word always expecting to receive from God a sense of his love and a supply of his grace. I would then, as I say, have a good hope that, through grace, ten thousand difficulties would never shake my perseverance in the faith. But if otherwise, there will be no persevering or abiding. I mention these things because, as far as I can

see, there is a great coldness and indifference increasingly gaining upon men's spirits as they attend the worship of God. There is not the life, spirit, courage and delight in it that there has been in the past; and if this is so, God only knows how it will end. This, I say, is the first thing that faith will do in this state, if we set it to work. If we would only make an effort to stir it up to find those supplies of spiritual life and strength in the paths of worship and the ordinances; if we would labour to overcome prejudices, and set ourselves against laziness and negligence. We would find ourselves like others who have been freed to a great extent from the worry of what the world can do to them. This is what faith can do for us, and this is what I am labouring to bring my own heart to.

(2) *Faith*, at such a time, *will bring the soul into such an experimental sense of the authority of Jesus Christ as to make it despise all other things.* I confess if it were not for the authority of Christ I would renounce all our meetings. They would have neither form nor majesty in them that they should be desired. But a deep respect for the authority of Christ (unless our evil hearts are betrayed by unbelief and weakness) will carry us through all that might happen to us. Faith works a double respect to the authority of Christ:

(a) *As he is the great head and lawgiver of the church*, who alone has received all power from the Father to institute all worship. Anyone who imposes on this authority usurps his crown and his dignity. All power to institute spiritual worship in heaven and in earth is given to Christ. What follows, therefore? 'Go therefore and make disciples of all

nations… teaching them to observe all that I have commanded you' (Matt. 28:18-20). Bring your souls to this work of
faith that we might do the things that Christ commands
us, who is the sovereign Lord of our consciences and has
sovereign authority over our souls. We must all appear before
his judgment-seat and he will require of us whether or not
we have done and obeyed what he has commanded us. Do
not only profess these things but make every effort by faith
to *affect* your conscience with this *authority of Christ.* You
will then find that all other authorities will come to nothing,
however much you may have to suffer for it.

(b) Faith respects the authority of Christ *as he is 'King of
Kings and Lord of lords'* (Rev. 19:16). It will respect him as
he sits at the right hand of God, waiting until his enemies
should be made a footstool for his feet, holding not only a
gold sceptre in his hand, 'a sceptre of righteousness' with
which he rules his church, but also an iron rod, to break all
his enemies in pieces like a potter's vessel. If faith is exercised
in this power and authority of Christ over his enemies it will
pour contempt on all that the world can do. You cannot be
brought before any magistrate or judge without Christ also
being present, greater than them all. He has their breath in
his hands, their lives and ways at his disposal, and he can
do what he pleases with them. Faith will bring in Christ's
presence at such a time, when otherwise your heart would
be full of fear and you would be left to your own wisdom—
which is just folly—and your own strength—which is just
weakness. But if you have a faith that is resting in the sense
of this authority it will make you like those three serene,

composed men of Daniel, chapter 3. Don't be surprised at the greatness of their answers and the composure of their spirits when they looked at the fiery furnace on the one hand, and the fiery countenance of terrible majesty on the other. 'Our God,' they said, 'whom we serve is able to deliver us out of your hand… But if not,'—if God will not give us a present deliverance,—'be it known to you, O king, that we will not serve your gods or worship the golden image that you have set up' (Dan. 3:17, 18). Faith will give us the same composed and resolute spirit, and with these we may be calm under the worst that can happen to us.

(c) In such a situation, faith *will bring to our minds the examples of those who have gone before us* who had the same testimony as ourselves, and the sufferings that they experienced on that account. When the apostle told the believing Hebrews (Heb. 10) that through all their trials, tribulations and sufferings, they must live by faith, they might have answered, 'What encouragement shall we receive by faith?' 'Why,' he answered, 'faith will bring to your minds all the examples of all those who have gone before you, who have suffered and been afflicted and distressed, just as you are now,'—which is the sum and substance of the whole of Hebrews 11 and the first verses of Hebrews 12. It is a great thing when faith reminds us of a past example. Let us then carry in our minds, by faith, the examples that are recorded for us in Scripture. There is the case of Moses which the apostle gives us. It is a wonderful example: 'Choosing rather to be mistreated with the people of God than to enjoy the fleeting pleasures of sin. He considered the reproach of

Christ greater wealth than the treasures of Egypt' (Heb. 1:25,26). He, even by the indistinct promises that he had to live by, endured the reproach of Christ. My brothers, take the prophets as examples of those who suffered, and consider how the apostles have gone before us, but do not stop with them, for there is a greater than Moses, a greater than the prophets or the apostles—one greater even than the cloud of witnesses; no less a person than the Lord Jesus Christ. Look 'to Jesus, the founder and perfecter of our faith, who for the joy that was set before him endured the cross, despising the shame' (Heb. 12:2). He endured such hostility from sinners against himself and is now 'seated at the right hand of the throne of God.' Faith, calling to mind these great examples, will give us strong support under all the trials that might come upon us. Where are we going? What do we hope for? We would wish to be where Moses is, and where the prophets are. But how did they get there? They did not get there by accumulating riches or by multiplying to themselves promotions and positions in the world, but by sufferings and crosses. Through many tribulations they entered into the kingdom of heaven.

(d) *Faith, at such a time, will receive from the supplies that Christ has laid up for his people.* Christ has specific provisions for suffering saints. They consist of two things. The first is his own special presence with them. He will be with them in the fire and in the water. Secondly, there is the communication to them of the sense of God's love to them. Our 'suffering produces endurance, and endurance produces character, and character produces hope, and hope does not put us to shame, because God's love has been poured into our hearts through the Holy Spirit who has been given to us' (Rom. 5:3-5). Faith will bring all these things to the soul. But your minds must be spiritual or you will not be able to exert an act of faith that will obtain this special provision stored up for suffering saints, and very few indeed reach this spiritual frame where faith is able to catch hold of these special consolations that Christ has for such souls. This is one way that we may live by faith in a time of trouble. Examine and search, therefore, at the beginning of difficulties, the sense of the love of God that faith gives, to carry you through those difficulties.

(e) *It is only faith that can encourage us by enabling us to look to the reward*. Moses chose to be 'mistreated with the people of God... for he was looking to the reward' (Heb. 11:25, 26). The slight momentary affliction which we undergo in this world 'is preparing for us an eternal weight of glory beyond all comparison' (2 Cor. 4:17). Who knows whether or not in a few days some of us may be taken into that incomprehensible glory, where for eternity we shall be amazed that we ever placed any importance at all on things here below? Faith will fix your eye on the eternal reward. We have, nowadays, a kind of faith at work that fixes the minds of men on this or that way of escape, and this or that strange providence, but we shall find that true faith will burn up all this as stubble.

(f) And lastly, *faith will work by patience*. The apostle tells us that 'we have need of patience, that, after we have done the will of God, we might receive the promise' (Heb. 10:36);

and we are to be 'imitators of those who through faith and patience inherit the promises' (Heb. 6:12).

This is part of what I had to offer to you and I hope it has proved timely and useful. It is the best I can manage in these times of reproach, scorn and contempt in which we find ourselves, with persecution approaching. Faith will find for us that efficacy, sweetness, power and advantage in our spiritual ordinances that will make us willing to undergo anything in order to be present at them. Faith will bring our souls into such subjection to the authority of Christ, as Head of the church and Lord over the whole creation, that we shall not be terrified by what man can do to us. Faith will remind us of the example of the saints of God, whom he helped and supported through their sufferings and who are now crowned and at rest in heaven. Faith will help to keep our eyes fixed, not on the things of this world, but on the eternal reward of another world, and glory in it. And faith will also work by patience when difficulties begin to multiply upon us.

Sermon 3
The use and advantage of faith in a time when Roman Catholicism is on the increase

The righteous shall live by his faith—Hab. 2:4

We are looking into how we may live by our faith with respect to those difficulties which we have, or may have to contend with in the days in which we live. The last topic on which we spoke was the way to live by faith with reference to all the reproaches and scornful contempt that are poured out on our form of worship, the order and fellowship of the gospel to which we hold, and the persecutions which we may have to suffer on their account. I now continue:

The second difficulty that we have, or may have to fight against is *the return of Popery to this land*. Half the talk of the world is on this subject. I have nothing to say to some from amongst ourselves, but I truly believe that those who manage the papal, antichristian affairs of this world are endeavouring to advance it in this country. I remember what holy Latimer said when he was dying: 'Once I believed Popery would never return to England, but I find that was not faith, but fancy.' I hope it does not prove to be so for many of us. Now what I am going to speak of is this: how we should live by faith at the prospect of this danger, and also when it does come upon us, should that occur. I will share with you a few things in which I school myself. If you have more supportive thoughts or a better light, I pray that God will confirm you in them.

(1) The first thing I would consider, and in which my faith rests, is this—*that there is a fixed, appointed time* in God's counsel when Antichrist and Babylon, idolatry and superstition, together with that profaneness of life which they have introduced, *shall be destroyed.* This is so certain that it shall never be altered. All the wisdom of men, all the sins of men, and all our unbelief, shall not delay the day. It shall most certainly occur at its appointed time. This time is accounted for in Scripture by days, by months, by years. Not in order that we should know the *set time* but that we should know the *certainty* of it: because if it only has so many days, so many months, so many years, then its date must be fixed.

We see this continually in the Old Testament. God said to Abraham, 'Know for certain that your offspring will be sojourners in a land that is not theirs and will be servants there, and they will be afflicted for four hundred years. But I will bring judgment on the nation that they serve' (Gen. 15:13,14). They did not know when was the beginning or the ending of this four hundred years, but they knew that at its end things would be as God had said; and 'on that very day, all the hosts of the LORD went out from the land of Egypt' (Exod. 12:41). Similarly, God threatened the Jews with a seventy-year captivity in Babylon: 'Then after seventy years are completed, I will punish the king of Babylon and that nation... for their iniquity' (Jer. 25:11, 12). The church did not know when the seventy years began or when they were to end, but this they knew, that at that very same day appointed, it should be as God had said. And so it proved to be.

The appointing and accounting of the time of the Man of Sin, of Antichrist, by days, and months, and years, is in order to establish our faith in the certain determination of that time, and not to satisfy our curiosity as to when exactly it shall be. But the thought that there is such a determined time is a great foundation for faith and patience. 'The least one shall become a clan, and the smallest one a mighty nation; I am the LORD; in its time I will hasten it' (Isa. 60:22). But if there is a fixed time for the fulfilling of this promise you might well ask, 'How can it then be hastened?' Well, because if you live in the exercise of faith and patience, it will suddenly surprise you. It will come when you were least expecting it: 'In its time I will hasten it.' 'I will not bring it before its time, however patient or impatient you may be, but if you exercise faith and patience I will so order it that it will be a sweet surprise for you.' And the waiting is itself a means of patience, 'If [the vision] seems slow, wait for it; it will surely come' (Hab. 2:3). When we know that it will come, when we know that there is an appointed time, and that its coming is certain, we have a firm ground for waiting patiently for it. This has been a great encouragement to me, and I share it with you. I can now believe in faith, with no need for speculations or surmising, that there is an appointed time in the counsels of God when he will pour out all his judgments and plagues upon the antichristian world, and Antichristianism will be destroyed and rooted out.

(2) Another thing that comforts my heart is this: *it is no less glorious to suffer under the beast and the false prophet than it was to suffer under the dragon.* The content of the book of the Revelation is predominantly these two things: the persecution of the church by the *dragon*—and *he* is conquered; the persecution of the church by the *beast and false prophet*—and *they* shall be conquered. The dragon was the heathen power of the Roman Empire, and it was a glorious thing to suffer under that power. They that did so are described in the revelation to John, 'These are the ones coming out of the great tribulation. They have washed their robes and made them white in the blood of the Lamb. Therefore they are before the throne of God, and serve him day and night in his temple; and he who sits on the throne will shelter them with his presence' (Rev. 7:14, 15). But of those who suffered under the beast and the false prophet, it is also said, 'They have conquered him by the blood of the Lamb and by the word of their testimony' (Rev. 12:11).

We consider those who won the liberty of the gospel and of the Christian religion by suffering against pagan powers, and who destroyed idolatry by shedding their blood, 'famishing all the gods of the earth' (Zeph. 2:11), as great and glorious martyrs. There have never been men more glorious than they. They make up the company of those who, with palms in their hands and a new song in their mouths, give glory to God (Rev. 7:9-12). But it is not any the less glorious to suffer under the beast and the false prophet (the second persecuting power), i.e. the papal, antichristian power, than to suffer under the pagan. The church has had to fight against this for many ages, and must continue to do so until the time comes when it shall obtain a complete and perfect victory over it. This is a glorious thing, and you must see it as such. If a time of martyrdoms at Smithfield should arrive again—if God should call us to that fiery trial, or to any other, whatever it might be—remember that to suffer against Antichrist is as great and glorious as to suffer against Paganism.

(3) Though our *persons* should fall, our *cause* will be as truly, certainly and infallibly victorious as that Christ sits at the right hand of God. When, amidst paganism, men of courage did not value their own lives for the sake of their cause, in this way the cause was continued. Now, whether your or my persons shall fall in this trial, yet the cause with which we are engaged will as surely conquer as that Christ is alive and will prevail at last. When the beast first rose up, it was said it 'made war on the saints… to conquer them' (Rev. 13:7). The poor Waldensians considered that they were those people prophesied of in this text, and said, as they were being butchered by the papal power, 'We are the conquered people of God, but there shall come forth conquerors.' When about to die, they knew and believed that their cause would conquer. And so, after Antichrist has conquered and prevailed over many for a season yet, at length, there will be a final encounter. 'They will make war on the Lamb, and the Lamb will conquer them and those… with him are called and chosen and faithful' (Rev. 17:14). The gospel will be victorious. This is the third thing that greatly comforts and refreshes me—that if God should give

me the honour, strength and grace to die in this cause, yet my cause shall be victorious, as sure as if I had the crown in my hand already.

(4) *The judgments of God shall come upon the antichristian world when they least expect them.* When the kings of the earth do not look for them; even when believers do not look for them; that is when they shall quickly come. The Holy Spirit tells us so expressly: 'her plagues will come in a single day, death and mourning and famine, and she will be burned up with fire' (Rev. 18:8). How is it possible that something of such position and power should be overcome by her plagues *in one day*? The reason is added: 'For mighty is the LORD God who has judged her.' Almighty strength will be put forth to accomplish it. And if this were not enough, the seventeenth verse tells you that it will take place 'in a single hour'. I do truly believe that the destruction of the power of this cursed antichristian state will be brought about by none of the means that we know of, or speak of, but that the strong Lord God will overthrow and destroy her by ways unknown to us. It may be tomorrow, it may not be for a hundred years. She herself, when it occurs, will not have expected any such thing: 'She glorified herself and lived in luxury… in her heart she says, "I sit as a queen, I am no widow, and mourning I shall never see." For this reason will her plagues come in a single day' (verses 7, 8). When she is boasting, destruction shall come. When the kings of the earth have no anticipation of it, then they shall cry, 'Alas, alas, for the great city… For in a single hour all this wealth has been laid waste' (verses 16, 17). And believers

themselves will be as the children of Israel were in Egypt. When Moses came to them they could not believe because of the cruel bondage that they were under. So will be the day that the judgments of God will fall upon Antichrist, the old enemies of Jesus Christ.

(5) We must consider seriously the greatness of *God's indignation against any who, in the least thing, compromises with Antichristianism* when it comes upon us. Revelation 13, verse 11, speaks of a beast that 'had two horns like a lamb and it spoke like a dragon... It exercised all the authority of the first beast.' (This, I think, is the pope.) He exercises a power answerable to the pagan power. And what follows? He 'causes all, both small and great, both rich and poor, both free and slave, to be marked on the right hand or the forehead, so that no one can buy or sell unless he has the mark' (verses 16, 17). The nature of the mark is not important, but the receiving of anything from him is to receive the mark; either on our foreheads, where we show it to all the world, or on our right hands, more secretly, where it may be shown when it is to our advantage to do so. And what then? 'I saw another angel flying directly overhead, with an eternal gospel to proclaim to those who dwell on earth, to every nation and tribe and language and people. And he said with a loud voice. "Fear God and give him glory, because the hour of his judgment has come, and worship him who made heaven and earth, the sea and the springs of water"' (Rev. 14: 6, 7). When Antichrist puts his mark on the hands and foreheads of the people, God, by his gospel, calls them from their false worship and idolatry. But what if they do not

obey? The ninth and tenth verses tell us that, 'another angel, a third, followed them, saying with a loud voice, 'If anyone worships the beast and its image and receives a mark on his forehead or on his hand, he also will drink the wine of God's wrath, poured full strength into the cup of his anger, and he will be tormented with fire and sulphur in the presence of the holy angels and in the presence of the Lamb.' Some will wish to say, 'Let us come to a sensible arrangement, and make some compromises, and put an end to these disputes.' No! Do so at your peril. God says that you shall drink of the wine of his wrath, poured full strength into the cup of his anger, and that for ever and ever. And I believe with all my heart and soul that this will be the portion of all the men and women of this nation that shall compromise with any return of antichristian idolatry among us. God will pour out his wrath against them.

(6) Remember that *if the trial comes, it will be a day of battle*. It is not for you, when preparing for battle, to be thinking of this way or that way for making an escape. No; it is courage, faithfulness and faith alone, that must be stirred up, or you will not be saved. All your wisdom and contrivances will not save you. Because it has come to the issue between Christ and Antichrist, it is the 'preparing of your minds for action' (1 Pet. 1:13) and continued 'resist to the point of shedding your blood' (Heb 12:4) against sin, that is your duty and your way of escape. Nothing will save you but faith, courage and faithfulness.

(7) There are suggestions in the Scripture that those who hold on strongly to God and to his worship, with faith, love

and delight, shall be preserved and saved. I am not saying that this is a certain promise, as all my other points have been, but I do say that there are suggestions which imply that those who, with quick and lively spirits, exercising faith, love and delight in God and his worship, those worshippers in the inner court of his temple, shall be strikingly saved at such a time. But I am afraid that few of us shall experience this, because I see so much coldness and deadness among us and among the churches of Christ. It makes me think that troubles will fall upon us all, in that we have so much need of them.

In conclusion, firstly, do not let your talk of *strange things* keep the thoughts of these matters from your hearts, because you will certainly be tried by Antichristianism before you die. We talk of new things and great events that we look out for in the world, and that Antichrist will be destroyed, but I do believe that he will test us severely in the meantime.

Secondly, beware of computations and calculations. How woefully and miserably have we been mistaken in this! We know the time is determined—its beginning and ending are known by God; but we must live by faith until all is fulfilled.

Thirdly, many of us have recommitted ourselves in covenant with God. Let us remember that we have taken the 'seal of God upon our foreheads' and woe betide us if we accept the mark of Antichrist alongside it.

This is all that I have to offer you with respect to living by faith under the apprehensions of those difficulties with which we shall have to fight at the entry of profaneness and idolatry. The world and hell are presently combined together in bringing these upon our nation once again.

Sermon 4
The use and advantage of faith in a time when true religion is declining

The righteous shall live by his faith—Hab. 2:4

I have now arrived at my last point, and with this I shall close, namely: how we are to live by faith under an apprehension of a great and sad decline in churches, in church membership, and in believers, and in the gradual withdrawal of God's glory from among us because of this. I wish to emphasize three points:

(1) That ours is a time of great declension, among church-members and believers throughout the nation and, indeed, throughout other nations also, wherever there are those who fear God.

(2) That this ought to be a matter of great trouble and trial to all true believers.

(3) And then, to show you how we are to live by faith at such a time; what it is that faith does to support the soul at such times.

(1) There are very many evidences that *we live in a time of declension*. I will point out a few of these:

(a) A sense of it impresses the minds of all the most judicious and careful Christians, those who are honest in their self-examination and take most notice of the ways of God. I have heard very many testifying of it. Complaints are heard from many in this, and neighbouring, countries that there is a great decay in the power of grace and the life of faith among all categories of believers. Some of them go even further in their evidence, testifying that they find the effects of it in themselves. They say that they find it difficult to maintain their former spiritual walk, that it requires much watchfulness and diligence, and that even then they fail in their attempts. And we must add that this is our testimony also, unless we are all absolute hypocrites, because I do not know how many times I have heard the same complaints in our own prayer meetings here. God has therefore placed a conviction upon the hearts and minds of spiritual, self-examining believers that churches, other believers and they themselves are experiencing spiritual decay.

This is the first evidence and, at such times in the past, we find that the best part of the church made that sad complaint because of it: 'O LORD, why do you make us wander from your ways and harden our heart, so that we fear you not?' (Isa. 63:17). They were aware that there was a judgment from God's hand upon them.

(b) The evident *lack of love* that is among churches, church members, and believers, is another evidence. I will not speak of the lack of love between churches, but as regards love between church members we have scarcely a shadow of it remaining among us. When men are related, when they are acquainted, when they agree in temperament and conduct, there is an appearance of love; and when they agree in theological faction and belief, there is an appearance of love. But on the *purely spiritual basis* of Christianity and church membership we have, I repeat, scarcely a shadow of it left. I remember how we used to be, when it was a joy to see one another's faces; when there was genuine love in all sincerity; love accompanied by sympathy, compassion and humility; love, indeed, with much delight. But this is dead in the churches, dead among believers.

(c) Another evidence of this decay is the *lack of delight and diligence in the ordinances of gospel worship*. These ordinances used to be a joy of heart to all those who feared God, but now there is so much deadness, coldness and indifference; so much under-valuing of the word, self-fullness, pride, and so much of a sense that we know everything; so little effort to tremble at every truth, by whatever means that will bring us to it. This all provides an evident testimony of the sad decays that have fallen upon us. Dead preachers! Dead hearers!

And all this is accompanied by two desperate evils (one of which I learnt of only recently, but on inquiry found it to be a far greater evil than I had supposed), namely, that men, who sense that others are not as enlivened and as quickened by our services of worship as they used to be, and finding the same thing in their own hearts (indeed, finding themselves growing dead and useless) have decided that such services have ceased to be useful and that they do not need to attend them anymore. This has happened to some who have for a long time lived soberly and diligently in their use of the ordinances. A godly and learned minister told me of many falling into this wrongdoing, a greater number than I would have thought possible. This is one of the evils.

The other accompanying evil is that this deadness and indifference towards our services of worship and our failure to bring our necks to the yoke of Christ in them, in opposition to all the arguments and devices of the flesh, has developed to such a degree that all attempts at reformation are useless. Men may make new arrangements and take all kinds of other steps, but this I know, that there is no way of reforming matters except for men to commit their hearts to return to God with more delight in his service. Some have stopped meeting together completely; some come with much reluctance—using their liberty, off and on, just as they please. Are not these things clear evidence of the decay among us? To me they are. I am not speaking of our congregation in particular but of the state of those churches in the land which I know of or have heard of.

(d) The last evidence that I shall mention of the decline among us is *our worldly-mindedness*, our conformity to the world and complacency. These things have been mentioned so often to you yet with no resulting reformation that they are now taken for granted, and I am discouraged from mentioning them anymore. But you may be certain: this conformity to this world and this complacent sense of security that is among us is firm evidence that the glory of God is departing from us. Ministers preach against these things but without making any impression upon the minds of men. We can hardly give one example of the least reformation. These things plainly demonstrate that we are all under great decays.

(2) An *awareness of this* general declension among churches, church members and believers *ought to exercise and concern our minds*. If we are content to think that everything is well with us because we are free from outward troubles, and we are not concerned about our low spiritual life, then I will not say that we are hypocrites but we truly are poor, low, dead, carnal, unspiritual Christians. It is a situation in which God is dishonoured, the world is offended and scandalized, the ruin of churches is hastened.

(3) But I will proceed to my main point: *how are we to live by faith in this situation?* What is the work of faith appropriate to this state? If things are as described, and our souls are burdened by our awareness of it, then what will faith do to ensure that we pass through this trial and live to God?

I will tell you something of what I have found by way of an answer. And unless you are directed by God to better things, then make use of these and improve them so that you may give glory to God by your faith, even in such a situation.

(a) Faith will remind the soul that, notwithstanding all circumstances, *Christ has built his church upon the rock*, so that nothing shall prevail against it. 'The promise,' says faith, 'extends also to the internal enemies of our souls—unbelief, deadness, and all other things—just as much as to our outward enemies.' Though we are all dead, helpless, lifeless, poor creatures; though we have preserved almost nothing but our outward order and have lost all our vigour and life of faith and obedience; yet Christ's church will abide and stand, and those that belong to him will be kept. 'Such and such have turned apostate,' said the apostle, 'but God's firm foundation stands, bearing this seal: "The LORD knows those who are his'" (2 Tim. 2:19). Here is my ground of hope, whatever the circumstances, however many fall, one after another. 'But God's firm foundation stands.' And it has a seal upon it: 'The LORD knows those who are his.' Everyone whom he has effectually called and built upon the rock, Jesus Christ, will be kept, whatever happens to the rest of the world. The sight of so many dangerous evils converging on the church of God from without, and so many evidences of a decaying spiritual state within believers themselves, will test our faith to trust itself to this promise of Christ: 'On this rock I will build my church, and the gates of hell shall not prevail against it' (Matt. 16:18). If you find that your spirit is at any time depressed by these things, and no other comfort is at hand, exercise your faith on this promise of Christ, and upon the sure standing of God's foundation—that he knows who are his, and will carry them through all these difficulties, and land them safe in heaven.

(b) Faith will also remind the soul that God still has *the fullness and portion of the Spirit*, and can pour it forth when he pleases, to recover us from this sad state, and renew us to holy obedience to himself. There are more promises with regard to God's supplying us with his Spirit to deliver us from our inward weaknesses than there are those with regard to his putting forth acts of power to deliver us from outward enemies. And God is able to do that inward work—reviving and renewing a spirit of faith, love, holiness, meekness, humility, self-denial and readiness for the cross. He is able, by one act of his power, to destroy all his enemies and make them the footstool of Christ, when he pleases. Live in the faith of this.

The psalmist says, 'He scatters hoarfrost like ashes' (Psa. 147:16, 17), and the result is a frozen ground; he brings death to it. But he also says, 'When you send forth your Spirit, they are created, and you renew the face of the ground' (Psa. 104:30). Similarly, there is a deadness upon all churches and believers to some degree, at this time. But God, who has the fullness of the Spirit, can send him forth and renew the face of the soul; can give believers and belief another face; not to compromise and trade, as is now done so often; not to be so high and haughty; not so earthly and worldly, as is seen so much now; but humble, meek, holy, broken-hearted and self-denying. God can send forth his Holy Spirit when he pleases and give all our churches and believers a new face, full of the life and flourishing of his grace in them. When God will do this I do not know, but I believe that he can do it; he is able to renew churches, by sending out supplies of his Spirit, whose fullness is with him, to recover them at the appropriate and appointed time. And more: I truly believe that when God has fulfilled his present purposes towards us, and has spoiled the glory of all flesh, he will renew the power and glory of religion among us again, even in our nation. I believe this truly, but not in the same way as I believe those other things that I have told you. Those I believe absolutely: that Christ has built his church upon a rock and that nothing shall ever finally prevail against it; and that God has the fullness and portion of his Spirit to renew us again to all the glory of belief and holy obedience. These last points are infallible truths that will not fail you, and upon which you may rest your souls to eternity. And if your faith in these truths will not give you support and comfort, I do not know what will.

(c) When your souls are perplexed over these things, your faith will say to you, 'Why are you cast down, O my soul?' Were not all these things foretold to you? 'In later times some will depart from the faith' (1 Tim. 4:1); 'In the last days there will come times of difficulty,' because there will be men 'having the appearance of godliness, but denying its power' (2 Tim. 3:1-5). It has been foretold to you that churches will decay and lose their first faith and love. 'Why are you surprised?' said our Saviour, 'I have said these things to you, that when their hour comes you may remember that I told them to you' (John 16:4). I was never so surprised as by this particular thing: how could it possibly be, that after so much teaching, so many mercies, trials and fears, after so many years with our lives in our hands, and so many glorious deliverances, that yet there should be decays found among us, and such a backward retreat? It is a great surprise to anyone who thinks about it. But as it was foretold that this is how it should be, 'let us live by faith.' God has some great purpose to fulfil in it, and then afterwards all will be well. 'When the LORD has finished all his work on Mount Zion and on Jerusalem,' *then* 'he will punish the speech of the arrogant heart of the king of Assyria, etc' (Isa. 10:12).

(d) And lastly, *faith*, if it is exercised, *will stir up every soul that possesses it to attend particularly to those duties that God requires at such a time.* This will then fulfil and complete our living by faith under such a trial. If we have faith, and exercise it, it will move us:

(i) to examine ourselves as to how far we have been caught up in these decays and have contracted their guilt;

(ii) to mourn greatly, because of God's departure from us;

(iii) to watch ourselves, and one another, carefully that we should not be overtaken by the causes and attitudes of this decay;

(iv) to zeal for God and for the honour of his gospel, that they might not suffer because of our mistakes.

In a word, faith will do *something*. For our part, we do little or nothing, but faith, when it is stirred up to exercise itself, it will do something. As to these special duties with respect to the decays that we have fallen into, O how little do we fulfil them in any way whatsoever. O that we might advise one another as to what to do; to help one another to recover from our weaknesses! This is what we are called to, what is required of us: to have faith in the faithfulness of Christ who has built his church upon the rock so that however bad things might be, nothing will prevail against it; to have faith in the fullness of the Spirit and Christ's promise to send him to renew the face of the church; to have faith in apprehending the truth of God, who has foretold these things; and to have a faith that stirs us up to attend to those special duties that God requires at our hands at such a time.

———————

PURITAN ♟ PAPERBACKS

PURITAN 🕯 PAPERBACKS

THE Banner of Truth Trust originated in 1957 in London. The founders believed that much of the best literature of historic Christianity had been allowed to fall into oblivion and that, under God, its recovery could well lead not only to a strengthening of the church, but to true revival.

Inter-denominational in vision, this publishing work is now international, and our lists include a number of contemporary authors along with classics from the past. The translation of these books into many languages is encouraged.

A monthly magazine, *The Banner of Truth*, is also published. More information about this and all our publications can be found on our website or supplied by either of the offices below.

THE BANNER OF TRUTH TRUST

3 Murrayfield Road
Edinburgh, EH12 6EL
UK

PO Box 621, Carlisle
Pennsylvania 17013,
USA

www.banneroftruth.org